·

Finance and Investing for the Long Run

Investing for Teens and Young Adults to Make the Most of Their Money.

Table of Contents

Disclaimer

No part of this eBook can be transmitted or reproduced in any form, including print, electronic, photocopying, scanning, mechanical, or recording, without prior written permission from the author.

While the author has taken the utmost effort to ensure the accuracy of the written content, all readers are advised to follow the information mentioned herein at their own risk. The author cannot be held responsible for any personal or commercial damage caused by the information. All readers are encouraged to seek professional advice when needed.

Investing is a risk, and you can lose money during times of high market volatility or bad individual company performance. No investment is guaranteed to make you money. And the best investments are generally personalized based on your individual cash flow and net worth. Ensure you consult a qualified financial advisor to ensure that you are adequately diversified and pick the investments that work for you.

Your Free Gift

We do want you to be best prepared for any inflationary shocks that might happen during this period. If you're trying to figure how to allocate your money, we have a $10000 free inflation portfolio below.

https://inflationportfolio.gr8.com/

The Importance of Long-Term Financial Planning

Planning plays a critical role in every sphere of life, and finances are no exception. Planning is the foundation for implementing a vision and allocating resources accordingly. It also helps to highlight unforeseen risks, therefore, helps in the development of feasible countermeasures.

Financial planning entails developing elaborate frameworks of managing money to meet life goals (Timmerman & Volkov, 2020). The developed approach is vital in controlling income, investment, and expenses, ensuring the planner can account for their finances. Financial planning also ensures that individuals allocate their income towards their priorities, underpinning the ability to achieve personal goals. A financial plan lays down an elaborate framework to ensure that individuals do not fall into financial problems and lower their quality of life.

Long-term financial planning is especially crucial in achieving long-term goals (Topa, Hernández-Solís, & Zappalà, 2018). It goes beyond the short-term circumstances, setting up young people on a pathway to implement their vision, augment financial growth, and increase their quality of life.

Long-term financial planning is vital to increasing savings. It gives teens and young adults insights into their income and expenses helping them optimize their spending and investments. While saving is possible without a long-time financial plan, it is less effective. Topa, Hernández-Solís, & Zappalà (2018), claim that the long-term financial plan augments the individual's ability to set saving targets and reach them. It also plays an integral role in creating a saving discipline since individuals have to follow a specific spending pattern. The long-term financial plan helps increase savings, therefore, increasing the chances of achieving more. For example, long-term financial planning plays a significant role in long-term projects such as building a family house (Garg & Singh, 2018). It enables individuals to save part of their income for an extended period, making their vision of building a house possible. With a financial plan, young people can save beyond their goals, and use the savings to accomplish other objectives.

A long-term financial plan guides young people through their lives' journey, helping them turn dreams into reality. A financial plan is important in creating wealth thus enhancing a person's living standards. The long-term financial plan is crucial in ensuring that one meets their daily needs optimally thus gradually increasing their quality of life (Timmerman & Volkov, 2020).

With a long-term financial plan, teens and young adults optimize their spending and support their lifestyles together with improved quality of life and mental health. The plan, therefore, sustains their quality of life while gradually increasing it. On this account, it is accurate to posit that long-term financial plans boost people's comfort while ensuring that their quality of life is maintained and keeps increasing (Lusardi, 2019). It helps a person attain peace of mind which is pivotal in augmenting the quality of life. With a long-term financial plan, individuals can use their funds to cover their expenses, splurge with their families, and invest for future goals without worry. Thus, the plan helps individuals manage their income optimally and with peace of mind.

The fundamental role of long-term financial plans is preparing for the future. Frameworks and approaches adopted to cater for future occurrences tend to foster preparedness. Long-term financial plans help account for future expenses and increase preparedness. There are numerous risks and unforeseen circumstances that require funds. For example, sickness, death, accidents, or job losses may require emergency-based approaches (Lusardi, 2019). Without emergency funds set aside to cater for expenses in such circumstances, individuals end up borrowing or facing considerable financial strain. Long-term financial planning plays an integral role in setting aside emergency funds to cater to unforeseen circumstances. It ensures that individuals can pay for varied funds on time without worry.

How Compounding Works in the Long Run

Compounding is a crucial tool for enabling savings growth and paying up debts. It is a formula used to augment the time value of money, increasing the principal amount and earned interest over preceding periods. Compounding guarantees that assets grow exponentially over time. Compounding differs from linear growth since capital gains or interests are invested in increasing earnings (Baid, 2020). Compounding makes the sum of money grow faster than when it earns simple interest. In cases of simple interest, the initial amount earns a particular interest over some time, and therefore only the principal amount attracts revenue. Generation of additional earnings over time is subject to the reinvestment of the initial capital and its earnings over a particular period. In compounding, the interest applies to the principal amount as well as the interest that the principal amount had earned earlier. It is therefore constructed as interest over interest and hence magnifies returns over a while. Also referred to as miracle compounding, this approach plays an integral role in growing savings or investments (Alikar et al., 2017). It assures individuals of continually increasing earnings over time since their investment earns them optimal returns. In the long run, compounding increases the amount of income generated through capital gains or interests on investments.

Banks and other financial institutions credit compound interest using compounding periods. These periods are daily, monthly, quarterly, semi-annually, or annually depending on the prevailing conditions. In the long run, compounding tends to increase the amounts invested exponentially. However, it is vital to point out that compounding is applicable for both assets and liabilities. Therefore, when applied to assets, it boosts its value more rapidly. It increases the asset's value due to the interest earned on both the principal and accumulated earnings over a while.

Compounding also increases the debt paid in the long run when applied to liabilities. In such cases, interests accumulate on the borrowed amounts and previous interest charges. The amount paid, therefore, increases since one has to pay the unpaid principal and compounded interest. In the long run, compounding increases the value of the debt and therefore, benefiting the lender while fostering disadvantages for the debtor. Therefore, it is accurate to argue that compounding increases the value of the principal amount in the long run if applied to assets or liabilities. The principle of charging interest on the initial amounts in addition to the interest incurred over a particular period accelerates this growth in the long run.

As mentioned earlier, compounding aligns with the principle of the time value of money. Due to money's earning capacity, the amount of funds one has now is worth more in the future. This theory enhances some of the core financial principles anchored on the notion that if money can earn interest, it is worth more the sooner it gets disbanded (Alikar et al., 2017). Consequently, compounding aligns with the principle of present discounted value, with the time frame playing an essential role in determining the future value. While the interest rate is also crucial, the compounding period determines the pace of the growth of assets hence augmenting the time value of money in the long run. The earning capacity of funds increases with the frequency of the compounding periods and the time frame taken to arrive at the final sum. For example, for one year, three compounding periods would increase the future value of the investment more than one compounding period in the same time frame (Baid, 2020). Similarly, funds that have gained a compound interest over three years earn more than those that earn for three months. Therefore, the longer the time frame, the more the earnings, and thus compounding has better earning capacity in the long run.

As indicated earlier, compounding earns interest for the initial amount and accumulated earnings over the same period. Compounding is crucial in finance; it is the foundation behind many investment strategies. Its ability to increase earnings significantly, in the long run, is pivotal in attracting investors. One of the most common applications is dividend investment plans offered by numerous corporations. This approach entails reinvesting the dividends on invested stocks to buy more shares. Reinvesting the cash dividends assures the shareholder of an increase in the value of the shares they hold in a firm and the consequent increase in value of their investment. It also assures them of a consistent increase in the cash dividends paid out by a firm in cases where corporations sustain their profitability. This example provides insights into double compounding, whereby on top of the growth in the number of shares from investing dividends into the stocks, the investor benefits from higher dividend payouts (Baid, 2020). They, therefore, continually increase the value of their investment sporadically, and the more they reinvest, the more the increase in value. In such cases, long-term investments mean that the investor earns more, therefore, making compounding, in the long run, a higher revenue earner than compounding in the short run.

To gain insights into the implications of compounding in the long run, it is vital to look into how money accumulates over time when earning annual compound interest. Compounding makes wealth grow faster; therefore, the more the frequency of the compounding period and the time frame of the investment, the higher the capital gains growth on the principal amount. Considering an annual investment interest return of 8% per annum and a monthly investment of 250 dollars, the returns provide elaborate insights into the impact of compounding and the period an individual saves. If an individual starts saving at the age of 25, they accumulate 878,570 dollars by the time they reach 65. If another individual starts saving the same amount under similar conditions when they are 45, they accumulate 148,268 dollars by age 65. On that account, it is accurate to posit that the difference of 20 compounding periods brings about a difference of 730,308 dollars (Alikar et al., 2017). The difference augments the notion that the compounding periods play a critical role in determining the amounts accumulated over time. It also supports the thought that compounding has better earnings in the long run. It is the foundation of the position that the earlier an individual starts to save, the better. Investing for more extended periods will ensure that compounding will be to your advantage in the long run.

Compared to simple interest, compounding has higher returns on investment. Taking into consideration the 250 dollars monthly investments within the 40- and 20-year periods, it is evident that the final amount of investment is smaller than when using compound interest. It is vital to point out that the investment during the two periods is 120,000 dollars and 60,000 dollars for the 40 years and 20 years investments respectively. However, the return on the simple interest is 313,362 dollars for the one who starts saving at 25 and 108,441 dollars for the individual who starts saving at 45. In the first case, there is a difference of 565,208 dollars while in the second instance the difference is 39,827 dollars. The difference underpins the notion that compounding is an effective approach to growing savings as compared to other techniques. Furthermore, the compounding period coupled with the time of investment is crucial in determining the return on investment. Chart 1 below shows the difference in returns between different periods with compounding and simple interest for the initial investments.

Figure 1: *This figure shows the difference in returns between different periods with compounding and simple interest at 8% per annum.*

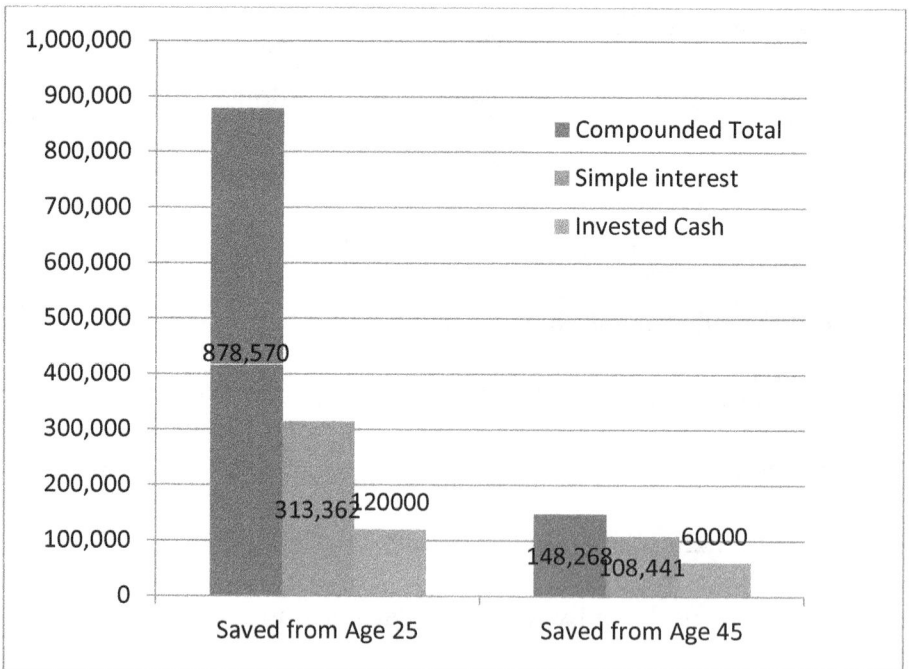

Inflation and Time Value of Money

The time value of money is a concept that holds that money held today is more valuable than that the same amount held on a future date. As a result, getting payment today is better than a later date. However, there is an exception when the money is kept in conditions where it gains interest. For example, when money is invested in equity securities or bank accounts that gain interest or debt instruments, it increases value (Alikar et al., 2017). Money invested in areas where it gains interest tends to increase in value at a future date as long as the interest rates exceed the inflation rate. Nevertheless, if kept in your pocket, it is less valuable in a year than the day in question. Therefore, the time value of money is subject to risk and returns. One has to risk, to gain returns in the future. It aligns with the role of compounding in growing the value of investments compared to keeping the funds in a condition where they do not gain interest. The Net Present Value is a crucial concept in elaborating the time value of money (Muda & Hasibuan, 2018). It helps provide insights into how time affects the monetary worth of things. It is also vital in showing the difference between the present and future purchasing power of money.

Inflation plays a major role in financial planning since it affects the relative value of money over time. Additionally, it has ripple implications for future prices of goods and services, thus affecting an individual's purchasing power. Inflation is considered as the change in the prices of a range of products over a particular period. It is the actual change in prices of consumer goods and can be used to determine future prices of goods and services. Inflation refers to the increase in the price levels. For example, 10% inflation indicates a 10% increase in the price of goods and services (Alikar et al., 2017). Inflation has adverse effects on the value of money as a medium of exchange. With increased inflation, the value of money keeps falling making it challenging to value goods. In cases of extreme inflation, prices of goods become more than the value of money, making it worthless. Calculated annually, inflation is important in developing monetary policies to maintain the value of money.

An increase in inflation increases the economy's volatility and affects how people trade and store value. High inflation makes it more difficult to use the money to store value, therefore, affecting the time value of money. The volatility associated with inflation is critical in debts at the same rate as investments. It erodes the actual value of debts, making them easier to repay (Muda & Hasibuan, 2018). This is the reason why in periods of high inflation, banks are less willing to lend money. They look to avoid situations where in the future, they make losses since people pay back debts when the money is worthless. In most cases, banks lend money with an interest rate higher than the inflation rate (Muda & Hasibuan, 2018). The volatility of high inflation rates makes setting the lending rates a daunting task because there is limited stability. Accordingly, it is accurate to posit that the present value of money is subject to inflation rates to determine the value of the same amount of fund at a future date.

In this analysis, it would be prudent to argue that inflation is among the significant determiners of the time value of money. Inflation has ripple implications for the present and future value of money, affecting investment and lending abilities. Another crucial element to note is that inflation erodes the purchasing power of money. The purchasing power of money refers to the number of goods it can buy in the future compared to the amounts it can buy in a period set as the base (Muda & Hasibuan, 2018). In most cases, it is the difference between what money can buy in the present compared to what it can buy in the days to come. For example, in 2014, one would purchase a movie ticket at 15 dollars; in the 1980s, they would purchase ten movie tickets with the 15 dollars (Kim, Anderson, & Seay, 2019). Purchasing power indicates that the number of goods purchased using a similar amount of money today is less than in the past and more than that which will get purchased in the future. Purchasing power, as a result, erodes with time, and inflation plays a critical role in this reduction.

Reduction of purchasing power over time aligns with the notion that the time value of money shows a significant reduction in the value of funds today compared to the past. However, the present value is more than the future value. The fact that prices typically go up in the future, amplifies the notion that inflation eats away savings (Muda & Hasibuan, 2018). The most notable example is if one keeps $10,000 under their bed today, this amount will be worthless 20 years from now. While the individual will not have lost their money, the value will reduce since they will only be able to purchase less. The same case applies when one keeps their money in the bank for a long time. While the bank interests offset the inflation, the interest growth fails to align with the inflation rates in some instances. Thereupon the saved amount loses value with time. To gain insights into this concept, it is important to point out that the dollar has an average inflation rate of 2.93% annually. Since 1980, the dollar has lost its purchase power by 2.3 dollars annually (Muda & Hasibuan, 2018). Therefore, $100, 41 years ago, had the purchasing power of 330 dollars today. On this ground, to purchase an item that cost 100 dollars in 1980, one will require 330 dollars. If individuals kept their $100 in 1980 and brought it out today, they would need to add $230 to purchase the product they would have bought with the $100 41 years ago. It is an indication that inflation eats away savings by reducing the value of the saved finances.

Understanding the role of inflation in the time value of money is necessary to make investments that consider these elements. The time value of money is imperative in enhancing the significance of investments since an individual can tap into money's earning capacity (Alikar et al., 2017). However, there is a downside with inflation playing a critical role in eroding the value of money over time.

Accordingly, considering the inflation rate is fundamental in ensuring that the invested funds increase their value over time rather than reduce it. It aligns with the principle of compounding interest with more extended investment periods, which accounts for increased value and growth of the invested funds. Therefore, when plotting the financial future, it is important to keep these principles in mind; they determine the growth curve of the invested funds and have ripple implications on the ability to achieve the set goals. It is vital to consider the inflation rates in a bid to make assumptions about the future spending power of money compared to its present value. It aligns with the principles of modified internal rates of return which are used to determine the actual value of return on investment considering the inflation rate (Muda & Hasibuan, 2018). On that account, it is accurate to argue that the time value of money and inflation are crucial determinants of investment returns. They help determine the most probable returns and thus play a central role in financial planning.

How to Create and Use a Budget

Budgets are fundamental in financial planning. They provide

revenue and expenses estimates, enabling individuals to optimally

project, understand, and manage their funds. In all activities that entail

spending money, budgets play a key role in that they ensure that individuals allocate their funds optimally to achieve their set objectives (Jones et al., 2017). In addition, they enhance control over finances since each person understands the percentage of funds used by each of their wants and needs. By keeping track of what you earn and how you spend it, budgets are pivotal in ensuring that there is the optimal management of resources. Budgets are also instrumental in setting goals and developing strategies to help achieve the set goals. They are also essential in measuring outcomes. They assist to elaborate the expected outcomes compared to the results in a particular period. By accounting for income and expenses, budgets also play a fundamental role in planning for contingencies. Budgets provide a platform to set aside funds to cater for unforeseen circumstances, therefore, helping mitigate risks.

Budgets are also referred to as spending plans. They specify how to balance income, expenses, and financial goals. They pump up the efficacy of financial plans for a specific period, estimating how much money one will make and spend within a set period. Budgets are crucial in accounting for the incoming and outgoing funds in a household or corporation. This accountability is vital in optimizing the efficacy of financial plans and ensuring that individuals achieve their set objectives (Tyson, Eric, & Tony, 2018). The budget also helps people understand if they have enough income to cater to the projected expenses. In cases where the money to spend is not enough, individuals apply planning strategies to prioritize their expenses and allocate money where it is most needed. Budgeting allows individuals to spend money appropriately since the spending plan allocates money for individual needs and aspects that are considered of high importance (Jones et al., 2017). The budget hence helps balance income with spending. Consequently, one is kept from spending more than they make. It is a crucial tool in keeping individuals out of debt and ensuring they achieve their preconceived objectives.

Budgeting plays a central role in augmenting control over money. It ensures that one can keep track of spending and has enough money to cater for expenses. It also helps individuals steer clear of debts and promote savings. By keeping track of where money is getting spent, budgets ensure that one eliminates unnecessary expenses to enhance the ability to achieve their set financial targets. They enable individuals to set realistic goals. With the insights on projected income within a given period, one can predict the goals they can achieve within this period (Tyson, Eric, & Tony, 2018). It is also a crucial tool in enhancing saving and debt elimination. Having a budget assists individuals in easily committing to saving and investing to grow their finances. Experts consider budgeting to be one of the most critical financial habits individuals can adopt. It not only enhances accountability but also plays an integral role in augmenting decision-making.

The process of creating a budget is subject to individual financial goals, estimated income, and expenses. Some prefer to write the budget by hand, while others prefer budgeting applications or spreadsheets. The steps adopted when creating a budget ensure that the tool augments financial management and the ability to achieve financial goals. Several critical elements are vital in developing a workable budget. First, the net income is vital since it helps highlight the money available for spending. It is important to note that is the money one makes in a given period minus statutory deductions such as tax, insurance, and retirement funds. Second, the estimated revenue is the foundation for operating budgets; one cannot spend amounts that are not within their reach (Fedosov et al., 2021). Additional revenue from other sources is also crucial. Finally, it helps come up with accurate income figures that should get included in the budget. The estimated income should reflect your take-home pay and thus play a requisite role in developing feasible budget estimates. With the overall income in mind, developing accurate budgets is less daunting.

Another crucial component is expenses. A budget has to indicate where the money is getting spent and therefore enabling appropriate allocation. In this sense, there are variable and discretionary expenses classified per individual needs. For example, utilities, food expenses, and other daily costs are classified as variable expenses (Tyson, Eric, & Tony, 2018). Therefore, they are given priority when allocating funds since without noting these expenses implementing the budget becomes an uphill task. However, it is essential to point out that streamlining these expenses to align with the available revenue is vital. One can change their spending habits to ensure they attain their financial goals (Fedosov et al., 2021). Consequently, individuals can cut costs to ensure that their spending conciliates with their income and financial needs. Discretionary expenses are those that individuals can do without. They include entertainment and meals at restaurants; while they are fundamental in enhancing their quality, individuals do not depend on them for survival. Budgets have to account for these expenses since they are part of their spending.

As earlier indicated, a budget is a significant financial planning tool. Its creation and implementation should reflect the set objectives. Vision plays an important role in planning when determining the most appropriate roadmap and frameworks to accomplish the ultimate goals. The vision is the focal point of the planning process and a crucial benchmark in determining whether the plan accomplishes the desired end goal. Similarly, financial goals are integral components in the budgeting process. They determine the length and extent of the budget coupled with priorities in the allocation of finances (Fedosov et al., 2021). Without well laid out financial goals, developing feasible budgets becomes a daunting task given that the budget maker has no explicit knowledge of the objective they look to accomplish. With clearly spelled out financial goals, developing an accurate budget is easily accomplished. Accordingly, the budgeting process should be tailored around the set financial goals (Tyson, Eric, & Tony, 2018). The budget should help individuals accomplish objectives aligning to a desired future position concerning finances. On that account, it is accurate to posit that while calculating the income and expenses is vital, coming up with feasible financial goals is pivotal in the budgeting process. It gives the budget direction while developing benchmarks to review the budget's efficacy over time.

Having understood the most critical components in a budget, it is essential to look into the budget-making process. The first step in creating a budget is collecting financial information, including financial statements and paperwork. This entails gathering up banking statements, utility bills, credit card bills, receipts from the past three months, and mortgage or auto loan statements. In cases of employed individuals, payslips are crucial in providing the required financial information. The next step is calculating income with the take-home pay in mind. This means that the income used must have accounted for all deductions; the most feasible approach is recording the monthly income (Jones et al., 2017). It is vital to note that for those who have a variable income, the most appropriate baseline income for the budget is income from the lowest-earning month. The last step in the first phase is listing all the expenses in order of priority. Categorizing fixed and variable expenses is important in ensuring that those costs that require immediate attention come first. It is also advisable to use information from past receipts to develop accurate estimates of the expenses (Tyson, Eric, & Tony, 2018). Including surprise expenses in the budget is highly advisable; it ensures that emergencies do not derail your budget. One also needs to assign spending values to each expense.

With the total net income and the total requirements for each expense category in mind, it is imperative to balance the two entries. The second phase of the budgeting process is a rigorous exercise of balancing the total income and total expenses. In cases where the income is more than the expenses, one is off to a good start since one can use the extra income to save or pay off debts. In other cases, the expenses are more than the income; therefore, developing an alternative approach to spending is the most feasible approach (Jones et al., 2017). It is critical to point out that the second phase of the budgeting process is fundamental. It entails bringing financial goals into play thus tipping the balance between income and expenses. During this process, elaborate decision-making stemming from individual preference regarding expenses and desired future financial position is necessary. It is the focal point of the budgeting processes since one has to align their income and spending with their set objectives (Tyson, Eric, & Tony, 2018). Achieving the set financial goals is subject to the budget maker's decision concerning how they spend their income.

In situations where the expenses surpass the income, developing feasible approaches to balance the two is vital. Cutting variable expenses is a viable solution to this situation. It entails eliminating discretionary expenses such as cutting out a gym membership, eating out less often, going for fewer holidays, or reducing spending on entertainment (Jones et al., 2017). Trimming fixed expenses is also highly advisable in a bid to reduce expenses. Individuals can take up approaches aimed at reducing expenses, including optimizing energy and resource usage.

For example, reducing food, water, and electricity wastage can help cut fixed costs by about 40 % (Tyson, Eric, & Tony, 2018). Another key approach in this phase is increasing income to help cover the budget's needs. When the expenses surpass the income, it is advisable to look for other income sources to help strike a balance between the two. This approach is also vital in ensuring that individuals achieve their set financial objectives since an increase in net income would play an important role in increasing the money available for spending. Furthermore, it enables the budget maker to achieve their financial goals. It is crucial to note that balancing the income and expense categories indicates that the budget is feasible (Fedosov et al., 2021). It helps account for the total income and spending on expenses, savings, and other financial goals.

Developing a budget is an uphill task and putting it to good use is the next phase. Budget implementation is as rigorous as the budget-making process. Using the budget to accomplish financial goals is crucial since it helps individuals realize the benefits of the budget-making process. It is imperative to indicate that one should make the budget work for them and not the other way round. One should use this tool to help achieve intended financial goals. Continuous tracking and monitoring of the spending highlighted within the budget is vital. It ensures that one aligns their expenses with the budget and achieves the set financial objectives (Tyson, Eric, & Tony, 2018). Additionally, tracking expenses helps keep the budget maker from overspending. The budget implementation process helps with the identification of problematic spending patterns or unnecessary expenses. The envelope system is a viable solution when people have issues tracking their expenses or following the budget outline. It entails putting money for different expenses in envelopes; once a particular envelope is empty; one must stop spending in that category (Jones et al., 2017). Taking funds from one expense category to help cover additional expenses is also a viable approach. Keeping an eye on spending ensures that the expenses are equal to or lower than the income.

Ensuring that a budget is highly flexible is important. The shifts fueled by the volatile business environments require a budget that can align with changing circumstances or shifts in priorities. It is, therefore, imperative to do periodic reviews to ensure that the budget is working for the budget maker's current goals and realities. A strict budget cannot account for life changes, for example, job changes, relocation, having additional children, or sickness (Tyson, Eric, & Tony, 2018). It is, then, less feasible and inappropriate in helping individuals reach their financial goals. Constant budget review is vital in making extra room or changing priorities to align with the current situation. It is the foundation of customizing the budget according to the financial situations and goals. The budget maker should adjust their budgets periodically to correct the underestimated or overestimated expenses. The review is vital in ensuring that the budget aligns with the financial goals and priorities. It helps to carry out a benchmarking activity with the budget maker, who, in most cases, will cross-reference the spending against the financial deliverables within a specific period (Jones et al., 2017). Therefore, continuous review is necessary for ensuring that the budget helps individuals reach their desired future financial position.

One of the most feasible budgeting approaches is the 50/30/20 technique. It is not only simple but also easy to use. The 50/30/20 approach has been recommended as one of the most suitable financing approaches for individuals looking to develop personal budgets (Tyson, Eric, & Tony, 2018). It enables people to develop a viable approach to meeting expenses and saving part of their income to meet financial goals. It is also an advisable technique in repaying debts and enabling individuals to enjoy a more balanced approach to aligning their income with spending. This budgeting plan posits that 50% of the total income should go into covering expenses. The 50% should meet personal needs, including the fixed and variable expenses. 30% of the income should cover wants, classified as discretional expenses such as entertainment and emergency funds to eliminate rigidity. It is vital to point out that budgets should help individuals enjoy life, and accounting for every penny is critical. Setting aside money for wants is pivotal in ensuring that one lets their money work for them (Fedosov et al., 2021). Finally, 20% of total income should go towards saving, with elements like retirement funds, stocks, fixed deposit accounts, and investment schemes taking center stage. The 20% that goes into saving is crucial in meeting financial goals.

Teens and young adults have an advantage over people of other age groups to understand budgeting. When they develop budgeting skills at a young age, they can continually enhance their competence and become experts in the long run (Generation, 2021). They can experiment with different budgeting techniques and develop frameworks to augment their ability to achieve their financial goals. In retrospect, when young people develop financial skills at an early age, they embrace financial literacy and foster a better quality of life in the long run (Tyson, Eric, & Tony, 2018). Budgets teach teenagers responsibility; they help them adopt a culture of spending money wisely. A budget is a crucial tool for instilling discipline when it comes to spending money optimally. Embracing its efficacy at a young age helps teens and young adults identify their spending patterns and eliminate negative lousy financial behavior. It also enables young people to develop insights on the most appropriate budget plan to accomplish different financial goals. Apart from enabling teens and young adults to spend money wisely and develop financial responsibility, budgets play an integral role in augmenting effective decision-making (Garg & Singh, 2018). Young people with practical budgeting skills make financial decisions that align with their goals in life.

Having the ability to develop a budget is a fundamental financial skill vital for lifetime financial success. It helps teenagers make wise decisions when spending their money and live within their means. It is a helpful tool in ensuring that one does not get into debt. It is also an important concept in money management since it has ripple implications for young adults and increases their wealth-making abilities later in life (Garg & Singh, 2018). During teenage years making mistakes when creating budgets is understandable. One can quickly correct these mistakes, identify lousy spending habits, and perfect their financial skills. Furthermore, developing budgeting skills at an early age helps teenagers commit to saving. They are influenced by the success of the milestones they make at an early age (Tyson, Eric, & Tony, 2018). Budgets play a central role in planning for holidays, buying the gadgets they need, and fostering financial freedom. Teens and young adults can therefore use budgets as their gateway to financial success over their lifespan development.

It is fundamental to point out that most young adults are tech-savvy. Statistics indicate that technology adaptation among individuals in this age group is over 88%. Using budgeting tools that capitalize on innovation will play a central role in augmenting financial management among young individuals (Garg & Singh, 2018). Spreadsheets are essential in this endeavor; they are simple to use and help individuals develop accurate budgets. Using spreadsheets, one can record their income, expenses, goals, and track their spending. It is a virtual platform that enhances the feasibility of budgeting among young people. The use of applications for mobile devices and software is also encouraged to underpin budgeting (Tyson, Eric, & Tony, 2018). The applications are vital in automating the budgeting processes and storing data that is crucial in analyzing budgeting trends. They help manage spending, monitor financial deliverables and keep track of the budget's efficacy.

Budgeting using technology platforms is also vital in setting up reminders and countering geographical barriers hindering budgeting processes. With technologically based budgeting, managing finances wherever you are and keeping accurate records is an easy task. Furthermore, it helps compare prices, track investments, and avoid financial mistakes that might derail individuals from their financial goals (Tyson, Eric, & Tony, 2018). Therefore, young people should capitalize on technology to develop their budgeting competencies and augment their financial management skills. It will play a crucial role in helping them make better financial decisions and put their budgets into practice. Additionally, technology-based budgeting is more accurate, helping them keep better track of their income, expenses, and spending patterns. Young adults can also use it as a point of reference in benchmarking their progress towards the set financial goals.

Strategies to Increase Income

i. Raise

Increasing income is important in reaching financial goals and enhancing the quality of life. With more income, individuals can spend or save more, have a better quality of life, and increase their abilities in wealth creation. One of the most common ways people increases their income is by asking for a pay rise. This technique is applicable for employed individuals with regular monthly income. Asking for a pay rise increases the salary paid by a certain percentage thus, increasing disposable income (Lazear, 2018). In some cases, this pay increase comes in the form of more overtime or working hours. In some companies, individual pay is subject to the number of hours employees work in a day. Thus, overtime is paid more than regular working hours. To balance productivity, some firms prefer increasing regular working hours and overtime to augment pay increases. The pay rise, in this case, is influenced by the employee's productivity. In other instances, one can ask for a pay rise due to the company's growth over time. For example, with increased profitability, employees can ask for an increase in their salary to motivate them to sustain their revenue generation ability (Ali & Ahmad, 2017). In such cases, a salary rise increases the employee's income and consequent ability to achieve more financial goals.

While asking for a pay rise sounds like a walk in the park, it's a delicate undertaking requiring good timing and approach. It is crucial to note that companies will periodically review their employees' salaries to determine whom to give a pay increase to (Ali & Ahmad, 2017). For this reason, taking the incentive to ask for a salary increase is a daunting task. It requires efficient preparation beforehand coupled with discretion. Dressing to look the part is vital in approaching the boss for a salary increase. Additionally, it is advisable to ask for a raise after an accomplishment is made. The process must also align with the firm's human resource management policies. Furthermore, aligning the pay rise request with a firm's financial trajectory is vital. Requesting for a pay rise with valid reasons is also a guarantee that the wishes get granted. For example, one can explain their financial situation with a sickness, new baby, or need to advance in education being valid reasons (Lazear, 2018). It is also vital to have alternatives in case the pay rise request is not granted. For example, one can ask to work for several days from home, attend a specific conference, or get new computing devices to enhance productivity. These alternatives should align with increased performance and an increase in the gross income for cases of individuals paid via commission.

ii.   Promotion

Promotions offer a variety of platforms to increase income. They are primarily in line with an employee's ability to offer more than they previously would since they have increased their experience. In other cases increasing education, skills, and competencies call for a promotion (Ali & Ahmad, 2017). It is crucial to point out that organizations have different methods of promoting their staff. The appraisal approach adopted by a firm determines the probability of an individual being promoted based on their performance. However, in some cases, one can ask for a promotion if they feel qualified for a particular position. Furthermore, with the changes in the organizational environment, positions are bound to keep coming up, creating room for promotions (Ali & Ahmad, 2017). Promotions offer a chance to work in a higher position and handle more responsibilities. With these responsibilities come more power and authority and, therefore, a salary increase. Promotions play an integral role in enhancing people's income since they increase their salaries, perks, and benefits. Once promoted, the monthly wage increases, other employment benefits such as sitting allowance, overtime, transport allowances, housing allowances, and medical insurance are also bound to increase. In most cases, promotions are automatically accompanied by an increase in income, while the perks play an integral role in increasing disposable income (Ali & Ahmad, 2017). The perks help in reducing the expenses and hence increasing the income indirectly.

Promotions come in several ways; the primary element in the different ways is the notion that they put individuals in a higher position than they were before. Apart from the promotion orchestrated by organizations when giving employees a higher position, individuals also climb up the corporate ladder through individual efforts (Ali & Ahmad, 2017). In most cases, it comes through searching for a different job in another company if there are no promotions within their organization. Once a person feels qualified for a higher position in another firm, they can opt to apply for such a post to promote their career. In most cases, individuals change their working environment when they feel another firm offers better rewards than their current firm or has a better working environment. In addition, job promotions are often an indication that a firm understands the employee's market value (Lazear, 2018). Finally, in some cases, promotions come without a pay rise, and therefore individuals have to negotiate with their employers to increase their salaries. In such cases, a 10% to 20% salary increase is the most viable pay rise. Promotions, therefore, increase job growth and hence play a central role in career advancement and personal development.

iii.   Side Business

While employment is a reliable source of income, it is highly rigid and guarantees little extra income, if any. For instance, having several side businesses plays a crucial role in increasing people's income. It helps individuals optimize their time usage and resourcefulness, which is crucial in adding to productivity (Cosenz & Noto, 2018). It is vital to understand that some side businesses flourish and later become the primary source of income. People, therefore, leave their employment entirely to focus on their side businesses since, in such cases, it brings in more income. The most common side businesses are those that stem from activities individuals love doing. For example, people with hobbies are passionate about their activities; once they turn them into a side business, they gain extra income. Hobbies such as gardening, painting, playing musical instruments, flower design, cooking, and photography have been known to provide extra income. In recent years Do It Yourself (DIY) crafts, gaming, blogging, and vlogging have emerged as well paying hobbies (Cosenz & Noto, 2018). Jewelry making, hiking, dancing, woodwork, and comedy are also feasible hobbies to increase income. They are therefore viable side businesses capable of increasing people's income significantly.

Apart from hobbies, individuals set up side businesses with the aim of making profits. They create businesses to increase their income and keep them busy during after-office hours. One of the most common side businesses is driving for rideshare companies since this job offers flexibility, and one can create time to pursue it. It also has fewer requirements since the same car individuals' use for personal transport can be turned into a taxi to help them generate extra revenue. Other side businesses have more requirements with those in charge having to employ others to take charge when they are not present. A person can set up a side business leaving a trusted person to run it on their behalf. For example, despite being employed, a person can start a café, fast food restaurant, or retail store to generate more income (Cosenz & Noto, 2018). In other cases, a car wash, saloon, barbershop, or massage parlor are efficient side businesses. Such ventures have the potential for growth provided the owner keeps constant control and employs a qualified and faithful workforce. The businesses generate extra income by adding more revenue on top of what they earn.

For those with tech-savvy skills, the internet offers a wide array of side businesses. In many cases, there is the element of freelancing that aligns with the ability to work during free time. Online side businesses require less capital investment and hence are highly attractive to many individuals. They rarely interfere with the main task, which is a critical requirement of a successful side business. Online selling is one of the most viable side businesses a person can venture into to generate more revenue. Individuals have numerous sites to sell products online, with Craigslist and eBay being the most prominent (Cosenz & Noto, 2018). Selling collectibles, old furniture, clothes, sneakers, or household appliances can make an extra buck. In most cases, people get these items for free, clean, and sell them, making supernormal profits. Recycling electronics, including computer parts, old phones, or electronic components, is also a viable side business. These items are quickly sold through websites like Gazelle (Cosenz & Noto, 2018). Holding garage sales is also a side business that can generate more revenue. What is considered to be of no value to one person may be of high value to others, and hence garage sales always generate revenue.

Offering services and amenities online is also a credible side business, with renting a house or part of the house through Airbnb being the most common approach. By renting a spare room, individuals generate more revenue. Another side business is providing online services such as tutoring via Skype, creating YouTube tutorials, or managing social media accounts for small businesses. One can also sell technical services via Upwork and Fivver (Cosenz & Noto, 2018). Creative individuals can also create a side business of designing logos, advertisements, or websites. Becoming a personal shopper is also a practical side business. It has emerged as a critical way of making money for individuals with limited time to shop and yet need specific items. As indicated earlier, the feasibility of side businesses is the ability to provide extra income without disrupting the day job. The primary advantage with online side businesses is flexibility; they offer a perfect opportunity to perfect skills while earning extra income.

iv.   Strategies for Teens and High Schoolers

Teens and high schoolers must realize that increasing their income is crucial in improving their quality of life. Additionally, as individuals grow older, their expenses increase. Thus, the need for extra income. While asking for a pay rise or getting a promotion at a young age is a daunting task, positioning your career for growth is vital. As indicated earlier, pay rise and promotions mostly come due to accomplishments or increased skills, knowledge, and competencies. Experience is also pivotal in increasing the chances of a promotion and pay rise. Teens and young adults should develop a continuous learning mindset to increase their knowledge, skills, and competencies and augment career growth. It is also necessary to work on their traits and attributes, with employee training programs and boot camps playing a central role in this endeavor. For high schoolers developing career choices is vital in helping them research and identify a mentor. It also helps them develop the skills and attributes required for a particular job to ensure that they are highly competent in their career life. It is the foundation for gaining experience early and getting a pay rise and promotion early in their careers. While they might not be eligible for promotions at a young age, maintaining the right mindset will guarantee a continuous income increase later in life.

Young people looking to make an extra income should think of venturing into business at an early age. Apart from developing the right mindset, developing the required character traits, and enhancing their skills and abilities, getting into activities to generate income is essential. It entails starting side businesses that do not interrupt their school work or family life. One of the strategies of getting an extra income is getting a part-time job. After school hours or summer holidays offer a perfect time to explore new job opportunities, and teenagers can learn and gain significant experience through such programs. It also helps them make money and therefore improve their financial independence from an early age. For those looking to become self-employed, babysitting is a suitable side business. It enables young individuals to generate income while balancing their school and social life. Pet grooming and dog walking are also feasible side businesses for teenagers; they enable them to make money during their free time. Additionally, these side businesses require minimal financial investments or skills. Teenagers and high schoolers can also tap into the digital space with social media platforms such as Instagram, Tiktok, Facebook, and YouTube to generate income. Selling on these platforms or becoming influencers can help young people make money during their free time.

Strategies to Reduce Debt Burden

i.   What is Debt and Why People Take on Debt? What to

Avoid?

When budgeting, aligning the income with expenses is crucial.

Furthermore, realizing financial goals is fundamental in enhancing the quality of life. When people spend more than they earn, they get into a financial crisis and require extra income (Greene, Greene, & Greene, 2021). Additionally, to realize financial goals that require capital investments, one has to either save money or get funds to repay at a slow pace. In such instances, debts are the best option; the fund's individuals borrow to repay at a later date. Debts are used to finance spending with emergencies, unforeseen expenses, or capital investments requiring more finances than the income. Therefore, anytime a person borrows money from another person or institution, debt is created. It is the money an individual or entity owes another through a legally binding process or consensus through word of mouth.

When one borrows money, they make agreements on the repayment schedule, and in most cases, the debt incurs an interest. In a forfeit, individuals are liable for litigations and punishments such as fines and a damaged credit score. The most common types of debts are mortgages, overdrafts, or student loans. Depending on the financial impact of debt on an individual, the borrowed money can positively or negatively impact a person's life. Good debts imply that they helped individuals create wealth, increase income, or get out of a financial crisis. On the other hand, bad debts have no return on investments or benefits to the person's financial life (Greene, Greene, & Greene, 2021). Regardless of the situation, it is significant to take debts that increase one's earning potential and boost their financial capabilities. As indicated earlier, people take on debts when their expenses exceed their income. In some instances, they look to purchase items that cost more than they earn. Others have no funds set aside for unforeseen circumstances such as accidents, sickness, death, or court cases. While these life events call for extra income to cover their costs, it is important to heed and not fall deep into debts. Other debts are crucial in enhancing the quality of life. For example, student loans help individuals learn and increase their earning potential (Greene, Greene, & Greene, 2021). Home loans help build houses and therefore eliminate the need for renting. Auto loans are also good debts since they help individuals to make capital investments and augment their movement.

As mentioned earlier, bad debts have adverse implications on people's financial lives. They have no benefits on their quality of life or financial health. People that get into and stay in bad debts often have lousy spending habits. They live beyond their means and, in many cases, are addicted to certain elements. With this in mind, it is vital to indicate that avoiding destructive spending patterns is crucial in mitigating debts. It is also advisable to avoid buying things one cannot afford, relying on credit cards, and focusing on wants instead of needs. Spending without a budget is also a recipe for disaster when it comes to borrowing money. It is vital to avoid impulse buying, interest-free financing, and buy now pay later arrangements. It is crucial to indicate that while getting into debts may be necessary for capital investments, sinking into bad borrowing and becoming dependent on loans is a lousy behavior. Debts drive people into bad credit scores; it also leads to depression and mental health issues. Therefore, avoiding bad debts at all costs is highly advisable for individuals looking to increase their financial health (Greene, Greene, & Greene, 2021). While debts can help one create more wealth and improve the quality of life, they can also become a source of misery and financial strain. Developing healthy borrowing habits is, consequently, the solution to the use of borrowed money.

ii.   **Strategy 1 - Refinance at a lower interest rate.**

Reducing the debt burden is a crucial process in augmenting financial health and freedom. As earlier indicated, debts can either assist in making life better or play a central role in making it miserable. Rather than living through life with negativity owing to the repayment of debts, developing strategies to repay them more peacefully is important. It is necessary to note that irrespective of their adverse implications, repayment of loans is a must. One of the most effective methods of repaying loans is debt refinancing. This helps reduce the debt burden by ensuring that the debtor has a more suitable loan repayment plan. Furthermore, debt refinancing is used to change loan repayment terms, making it less strenuous for the debtor (Ottaviani & Vandone, 2018). It is crucial to point out that one of the most common effects of bad loans is harming the net income. They limit a debtor's ability to meet their expenses and achieve the set financial goals. In some cases, the debts have implications on the debtor's quality of life. The obligation towards repayment takes up most of the income they would use for other necessities. Refinancing is, therefore, an integral approach in this case; it helps the debtor pay up the loan with less strain. On the other hand, it assures the lender that the debtor will repay the loan without default. It, therefore, creates a win-win situation for both parties.

Debt refinancing entails the replacement of a financial obligation with another obligation but under different terms. It involves taking up a new loan to repay existing debt. Therefore, the debtor is left paying a new loan under a different repayment schedule and new interest rates. Several factors influence the debt refinancing process (Spader, 2021). The terms and conditions are subject to the state or country debt policies or a nation's credit rating. Additionally, the borrower's creditworthiness, banking regulations, and level of financial distress also affect the refinancing process. Economic factors such as political environments, currency stability, and the projected inherent risks can also influence the refinancing process significantly. These elements play a pivotal role in developing the debt refinancing plan and the consequent repayment options. While many loans offer refinancing options, providing the borrower with more favorable terms aligns with a lender's profit-generating abilities (Ottaviani & Vandone, 2018). The primary reason borrowers refinance their loans is to get more affordable debts. It is, however, vital to note that the lender's schedule does not change; despite providing a better repayment plan, their end goal is profit generation. Teenagers and young adults have to realize that refinancing is not an escape plan, rather a way of prolonging the debt repayment processes to give the borrower more breathing room.

There are several notable advantages associated with debt refinancing. One of the most significant benefits is debt repayment with a lower interest rate. Reduction of the interest rates in most cases comes with an increase in the debt repayment period. The new debt helps clear the old loan, and the repayment period is prolonged to reduce the monthly installments and the interest rates (Spader, 2021). Therefore, the debtor ends up paying less for a more extended period and clearing their debt with time. It is necessary to point out that the new arrangement is more favorable since it does not take up a large portion of their net income. In other instances, refinancing plays a central role in enabling the borrower to avoid the penalties associated with defaulted repayments. Refinancing is also used to consolidate debts into one loan, enabling the borrower to develop a more elaborate repayment plan. It, hence, makes the debt more affordable and therefore reduces the debt burden on the borrower. Finally, it is indispensable to point out that debt refinancing looks to develop a more convenient repayment structure (Spader, 2021). Therefore, in other cases, borrowers prefer adopting an arrangement that enables them to repay their debts faster. They look to avoid the overall extra costs of more extended repayments and accrued interests.

Teenagers and young adults should consider refinancing to reduce their debt burden. This approach has more benefits than limitations. For example, they can use the technique to refinance their student loans by consolidating the debts into one package. Therefore, instead of repaying the different student loans with different interest rates, they pay a consolidated debt with one interest rate. The approach makes student loans less of a financial burden in the early years of their career life. Another crucial application of this approach is repaying credit card loans. It is important to point out that credit card loans accrue monthly interests, which are expensive in the long run (Ottaviani & Vandone, 2018). Many credit card users take up personal loans to pay up the credit card loans, reducing the costs associated with monthly interests. This type of refinancing is vital in reducing loan costs. Mortgages, auto, and business loans also have refinancing options to enable the borrower to pay the debt in more favorable terms. Understanding these aspects is crucial in enabling young adults to get out of debt burdens and ensure that loan repayment has minimal implications on their future financial health.

iii.   Strategy 2 - Debt Snowball Method

The process of debt repayment is often daunting due to the financial strain it has on the borrower. In many cases, the motivation and willingness to repay a loan are lacking, especially when the debt does not achieve its set objectives. However, debt repayment is obligated by law and has significant implications on the borrower's credit score. In cases where one has several debts, repaying them at once is a tall order. The debt snowball method comes in handy in such instances, enabling the borrower to reduce their debt burden procedurally (Gathergood et al., 2019). This technique entails repaying debts starting from the smallest to the largest. It capitalizes on the momentum augmented by the gains realized by repaying the small debts to completion. The accomplishment associated with repaying these debts plays an integral role in influencing the borrower to repay the more considerable debts. Furthermore, it capitalizes on the momentum gathered from completing the smaller debts. Therefore, the debt snowball method is vital in reducing the debt burden by helping the borrower stay motivated to the cause.

Several critical steps augment the success of the debt snowball method. First, it is important to highlight that the technique replicates the movement of a snowball on the ground. It gathers speed as it moves along. Young adults and teenagers looking to use the snowball method should list their debts from the smallest to the largest regardless of their interest rates. The next phase is making minimum payments on loans except the smallest. They should then pay the highest amount they can on the smallest loan (Gathergood et al., 2019). The snowball approach entails repeating these steps until all the debts are paid. The technique helps reduce the debt burden progressively while ensuring that the borrower repays their loans and interests to the fullest. By capitalizing on the achievements of completing the smaller loans, the borrower pays their obligations until they become debt-free. Young adults should embrace this method to reduce their loan burden and get out of debt with time.

To understand this concept, it is crucial to look into an individual with several credit card loans. It is crucial to indicate that the primary goal of using the snowball technique is reducing the debt burden by capitalizing on progressive success (Ottaviani & Vandone, 2018). Considering the smallest debt is a critical element in the case of an individual with credit card loan balances of $4000, $2000, $1000, and $3000. Irrespective of the interest rates incurred by each loan, the debt with the least amount of minimum payment should take priority. In this example, the minimum payment for the $1000 debt is $50, $2000 is $65, $3000 is $75, and $4000 is $100. If the person allocates $1000 towards debt repayment each month, they first need to clear the minimum balances for each debt. Therefore, during the first month, they pay the minimum amount for every debt, which amounts to $290. The snowball method requires that the borrowers repay the smallest debt first, and therefore the remaining 710 dollars should go towards repaying the 1000-dollar loan. Having paid $760 in the first month, the second month will see the borrower clear the $1000 debt and remain with $520. This amount will go towards the $2000 loan and repay $ 650 within the first two months. Having completed the $1000 debt and cleared 33% of the $2000 debt within two months, the borrower will

drastically reduce their debt burden and increase efforts towards debt

repayment. In the third month, they should pay the minimum balances

for all loans, and the remainder should go towards repaying the $2000

debt. They should repeat this process until all debts are repaid. This

example provides the real-life application of the debt snowball method

in reducing the debt burden.

iv.   **Strategy 3 – Cut credit cards for those who have bad habits**

Accumulated monthly obligations from credit card loans can

sink individuals into debts. Teenagers and young adults should avoid

impulse buying using credit cards or buying stuff for personal

gratification. Additionally, depending on credit cards to maintain a

lifestyle, one cannot sink people into a financial crisis. The same

applies to individuals who have multiple credit cards and hence

accumulated debts from different avenues. Such individuals should

adopt a cash-only approach to avoid using credit cards. To reduce their

debt burden, they should also consider having one or two credit cards

only. They should also avoid paying the minimum amount on credit cards since it leads to the accumulation of debts (Murugiah & Mohd Rashid, 2017). Shopping as per the budget is highly advisable as it helps in reducing the probability of using credit cards and getting into debt. It ensures that individuals only pay for what they need, thus helping develop sacrificial characters. Rather than using credit cards, it is better to use debit cards since they do not incur interests or sink people into bad debts. For those without financial discipline, steering clear of credit cards will go a long way in reducing their debt burden.

How Much Cash Should You Have?

i. Depends on how stable the economy is/ risk of inflation

Comprehending how the economy works and how market forces influence your assets is the initial step towards safeguarding your financial status. If you follow financial news, you have heard financial gurus deliberating on the inflation rate all around the globe. Although these experts make inflation sound like a thing to worry about, they fail to expound on the basics, including how it impacts the financial position of people. Inflation is when the prices of goods and services increase throughout the nation. Here, the purchasing power of a person declines when prices increase. For example, in 1950, the value of a single dollar was stronger as the average house went for around $7,354 (Nofsinger, 2017). However, wages and prices have increased over the decades, making the value of a single dollar decline significantly. This is a clear example of inflation.

With time, inflation can diminish the value of savings since prices increase in the future, especially with cash. For instance, if you keep $10,000 in your house, the money will not buy much in the next two decades. Although you will not lose money, you will have a lower net worth since inflation decreases your buying power. In case of high inflation, the bank gives you a higher interest rate. However, your savings may not increase rapidly enough to offset the inflation loss. For example, if you have $100 in a savings account that pays a 1% interest rate, you will have $101 after one year in your account (Long, 2016). However, if the inflation rate is 2%, you will require $102 to have the same purchasing power you commenced with. Here, you have gained a dollar but lost purchasing power. Similarly, when savings fail to grow at the same pace as inflation, you will lose money.

Moreover, inflation affects investments. For investments with yearly returns, such as ordinary bonds, inflation harms your earnings. On the other hand, inflation affects stocks differently. When the economy is stable, inflation is generally high. Here, firms sell more, raising their share price. However, firms have to pay more for inputs and to their workers, which reduces their returns. The impact of inflation on a stock relies on the performance of the organization. On the other hand, precious metals such as gold perform relatively well during high inflation. When the value of the dollar declines, it costs more to purchase the same amount of gold.

How can you plan for inflation? Inflation is one of the primary reasons most individuals do not use banks since it can reduce the value of their savings. As a result, some people favor putting their cash in higher-growth investments, such as stocks since they are less affected by inflation. Here, an individual must consider having a portfolio that reduces the impact of inflation, such as fixed investments. Although inflation is impossible to avoid, planning for it and enacting a strong investment approach can help reduce the effect of inflation on your financial plan. Another strategy is to rethink the emergency fund. It is difficult to keep a lot of money in a savings account when its value may decline quickly. Consequently, many financial experts recommend dumping your money when inflation is increasing. In addition, one can choose to review debt balances. One can repay their debt with cash that is worth less than the amount they borrowed. Similarly, one can get ready for inflation by de-risking their portfolio while continuing to invest, adjust their emergency fund approach as required, and move away from variable-rate debt.

ii.   Depends on your personal situation

Everyone must have a safety net to fall back when the unanticipated occurs. However, we are different. This means that the amount of money one should keep depends on their circumstances and lifestyle. Financial advice is not a one-size-fits-all, and any individual who offers you a fixed number of how much cash all of us should have is selling you short. Hence, when individuals ask how much money one should hold, it should not surprise you that there is no single number. Here, we must consider various factors before determining how much cash one should have. We need to keep cash to cater for regular bills, discretionary spending, and an emergency fund. Half of the world's population utilizes only cash. Cash is predictable, reliable, and boring. It should be readily accessed when one needs it.

Cash is the money individuals use to cover their living expenses. It is the money in the checking account. Cash should be grounded on fixed expenses, such as utilities, groceries, and rent, and the amount of money left for other activities like movies and date nights. Expenses are not fixed, which means that the amount of cash one has, keeps changing. For most of us, there is little or no money left after covering our living expenses. Hence, we should ensure that we live a lifestyle that one can afford. Here, keeping a cash reserve of around $2-3K will help you cater for expenses and prevent you from being caught off guard (Long, 2016). Extra cash should be allocated to short and long-term goals.

Here, one should keep an emergency fund for unexpected expenses. This is cash that helps an individual to survive unforeseen job transitions, diseases, or other unexpected events. There are many recommendations on how much the emergency fund should contain. For some, it should be six to twelve months of the monthly expenses, while others recommend three months of fixed expenses. Financial experts recommend keeping the emergency fund in the bank to gather interests and other benefits, especially high-yield savings. However, such a fund will be affected by inflation in the long run. An emergency fund is not something that requires you to keep adding unless fixed expenses change. The goal is to survive tough times and gather money for savings and investments.

Short-term goals are things that you want to accomplish in the next one-three years. They include putting a down payment for a house and taking a vacation to Malaysia. A short-term goal is anything that costs a lot of money and occurs in the next three years. It is the money one requires to utilize soon. On most occasions, this money stays in cash since individuals do not want to mess with it.

Medium-term goals are objectives one wants to finish more than three years from now but before retirement. They include buying a house and getting married. There is a connection between short and medium-term goals, which vary from individual to individual and throughout a person's life. Most people have fewer medium-term goals since they lack fixed plans that stretch for an extended period. Hence, this is the money one can invest in liquid aspects.

Therefore, if your goals go beyond five years, the money should be invested in the stock market, such as stocks, bonds, or mutual funds. Nonetheless, the money is not for funding your retirement account. The aim is to ensure that you can sell without consequence when it is time to fund your goal. Here, investing the money in money markets allows the money to grow without incurring extra taxes such as taxes for withdrawing prematurely.

iii. General Recommendation in 6 Months of Living Expenses

The first aspect that determines a personal situation is the household expenses. For example, a young individual in a shared-rental room outside London will be able to cope with much less than an individual with children in private school and a huge mortgage. In addition, earning more can lead to more spending, which means that a bigger proportion of wealthier households goes into non-essentials, especially holidays and restaurants (Long, 2016). Hence, your monthly spending should depend on your monthly expenses.

The first step is to formulate your expenses. One needs to check the actual spending and what one is spending on. Once you identify the spending, one needs to decide which expenses should be catered for in case of job loss. Here, divide the spending into three sections as shown below in figure 2.

Figure 2: *Break down of spending in sections*

Essential	Comfortable	Non-essential
Rent/mortgage	Internet	Eating out/takeaw
Food	Education costs	Gym membership
Utility bills & council tax	Clothing	General shopping
Medicines/healthcare	Transport costs	Holidays
Insurance	Mobile phone	Pension/savings
		Alcohol
		Entertainment

Source: (Long, 2016)

We are all different. The decision over which bills to cater for will rely on the compromises one is willing to endure during tough times. It depends on the savings goal one is seeking to realize. Most of the use must aim for a minimum of three to six months' worth of expenses when working and four years of expenses at retirement. Moreover, everyone commences with a budget. Failure to have an appropriate budget may lead to money issues. Hence, if you lack a budget, it is high time to draft one and start managing your money effectively. A budget is an approximation of income and expenses over a, particularly future period. A personal budget is a summary that compares and monitors one's income and expenses for a defined time, normally one month. It will help you see how much money you expect to generate and how much you spend. It is a way of realizing your financial goals and tracks your spending habits. The first step of formulating a budget is to gather your financial information. Here, look at the bank statement, utility bills, and other financial aspects. Then, calculate your income and create a list of monthly expenses. Later, determine your fixed and variable expenses and calculate the monthly wages and expenses. Then, make relevant adjustments to make the income to be at least equal to or more than the expenses. Finally, review and adjust the budget since circumstances change.

There are various ways of creating a budget. We have the 50/30/20 rule, where an individual ignores a sophisticated budget and thinks of the money as sitting in a basket (Brittney, 2021). The first basket is for fixed expenses, which are costs that do not change. These expenses include bills, such as internet, electricity, and mortgage. These expenses must be covered and there is nothing one can do about them. In most scenarios, fixed expenses should be around 50% of the monthly budget (Brittney, 2021). The next basket is for discretionary money, which is the money utilized on wants rather than needs. Some individuals include food in this basket. This means that one has many choices when it comes to discretionary money. One can choose to purchase a famous brand or to buy affordable items. Movie tickets, new gadgets, and philanthropy work fall in this category. The general rule is that 30% of the income should fall in this basket, but financial experts assert that this proportion is too high. The last basket is for financial goals. 20% of your income should go to realizing your financial goals. This basket is crucial for your future and includes savings and retirement funds, such as IRAs. Therefore, if you lack an emergency fund, this 20% should be directed into creating one. Another budget formulation strategy is Dave Ramsey`s Method as shown in figure 3.

Figure 3: *Dave Ramsey's budget percentages.*

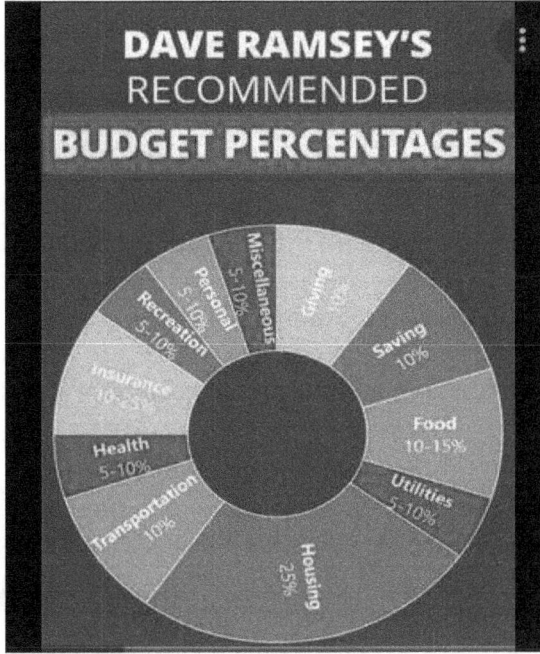

DAVE RAMSEY'S
RECOMMENDED
BUDGET PERCENTAGES

Miscellaneous 5-10%
Giving 10%
Personal 5-10%
Recreation 5-10%
Saving 10%
Insurance 10-25%
Food 10-15%
Health 5-10%
Utilities 5-10%
Transportation 10%
Housing 25%

Source: (Brittney, 2021).

Apart from the monthly living expenses and discretionary money, a larger percentage of the cash held should be part of the emergency fund. From the above strategy, the cash for the fund should come from the part of the budget dedicated to savings: around 20% or Ramsey's 10%. However, everyone has a different opinion on the amount of money one should keep in this fund. Financial experts recommend a cash reserve for an emergency that is equal to six months' expenses. For example, if you require $4,000 for monthly expenses, save $24,000. According to Nofsinger (2017), one should keep eight-month emergency funds since it takes a lengthy period for an ordinary person to get work.

The primary concern when dealing with the emergency fund is whether the fund should be kept in the bank. Some professionals suggest keeping huge emergency funds in an investment account with fairly safe shares to earn more interest than one would get in a savings account. On the other hand, some are concerned with the safety of the fund. The primary issue is that the money should be immediately accessible when one requires it. Hence, one should create an emergency fund before committing their savings towards retirement and other financial goals. The objective is to establish a fund of three months' expenses, then dividing the funds between savings and investment. Later, the savings should go towards retirement and other aspects.

H. How Much Risk Should You Take?

Risk tolerance is the degree of unpredictability in investment returns that an investor is ready to endure in their financial goals. Risk tolerance is a fundamental aspect of investing. Individuals should have a practical comprehension of their capacity and readiness to endure huge swings in the value of their investments. If one undertakes a lot of risks, one might panic and dispose at the wrong time. Risk tolerance is linked to age. However, this is not the only determining force. Young individuals have a lengthier time horizon and are frequently asked to undertake larger risks than older people. In addition, greater risks tolerance is frequently equated to equities and equity funds and ETFs, while lower-risk endurance is linked to bonds and bond funds. Apart from age, life goals and financial goals influence the amount of risk an individual can tolerate. Other factors include the time horizon one has to invest, future earning ability and the presence of other assets like pension and inheritance.

There are three types of investors when it comes to risk tolerance; aggressive, moderate, and conservative. Aggressive investors are market-savvy individuals with an extended comprehension of securities and their value. As such, this enables these people and institutions to buy highly volatile tools, like small-firm stocks that can crash to zero or options contracts that can terminate worthlessly. While keeping a foundation of riskless securities, aggressive investors attain maximum returns with maximum risk. On the other hand, moderate investors tolerate some risk to the principal but implement a balanced strategy with intermediate-risk time horizons of between five to ten years. Moderate investors frequently utilize the 50/50 arrangement which entails combining large-firm mutual funds with less unstable bonds and riskless securities. A common approach entails investing 50% of the portfolio in a dividend-paying, growth fund. Additionally, conservative investors are ready to tolerate little or no instability in their investments. Here, retirees spend a lot of time establishing a portfolio that is not ready to facilitate any kind of risk to their principal. These individuals target instruments that are guaranteed and highly liquid.

i.   Depends On Age and Life Goals

Our relationship with money starts at an early age when we see close ones exchanging cash for products and services we like. The power of money grows when we receive our first allowance or paid tasks. These childhood and adolescence activities foster our habits and beliefs that last throughout our entire lives. The challenges increase as we head to adulthood and are encouraged to take loans to purchase things, such as cars. Our parents and guardians set the pace for investment objectives early in our lives, teaching us to postpone satisfaction until we can fill the piggy bank, enabling the money to be used to purchase clothes and electronic gadgets. The close relationship between investment and lifestyle becomes more complex with age.

Investment goals are spread into three divisions, depending on age, income, and perspective. Age can further be split into three parts: young, middle-aged, and old. However, these categorizations frequently miss their mark at the correct age, with middle-aged individuals seeking to invest for the first time or old individuals mandated to thoroughly budget, implementing the self-restraint they lacked when they were young.

Income offers the inherent beginning point for investment goals since one cannot invest what one does not have. The first job is a call for all young individuals to make decisions about saving money and making lifestyle decisions that mandate balanced growing affluence with delayed gratification. However, it is normal to experience challenges during this time, such as getting stuck in a costly rental or a car loan that is larger than one can afford to pay. Perspective refers to the playing field on which we live our lives and the choices we make affect affluence management. For most individuals, family planning is the topmost priority. For couples deciding the number of children they want, their neighbourhood preference, and the amount of income required to realize those goals. Similarly, career expectations play a vital role in these calculations, with highly educated individuals embracing increased earning power and while others are trapped in jobs where they cannot advance, mandating them to cut back to meet their living expenses.

Investment goals are moving targets for most people, with carefully formulated plans encountering challenges inform of layoffs, unanticipated pregnancies, and health problems. These unanticipated hurdles necessitate a dose of practicality when selecting budget allocations. Fortunately, it is never too late to become an investor. Although feat can dominate when one is older, you only need to add a sense of urgency to wealth management. All investments begin with a little cash set aside regardless of your age, income, or perspective.

However, investing for decades has a major advantage since expanding wealth allows individuals to enjoy the fruits of saving behaviors.

Financial planning is the key to financial independence that guarantees future security for the future. It comprises both immediate and long-term benefits. A well-established financial plan enhances efficient tax management and integrates provisions for insurance and well-being. There are three primary aspects that a crucial in financial planning: protection, investment, and credit. Money is either preserved for financial protection, invested for capital appreciation, or used in credit activities for varying expenses. As individuals age, their financial goal strategy will vary with changes in income and risk tolerance. At the start of one's professional journey, a person needs to concentrate more on credit options for meeting prominent life goals. Young individuals come out of college and look for opportunities to accomplish their dreams and fulfill their responsibilities. These individuals must create a budget and adhere to it. At this stage, their investment appetite is low since young people are filled with the eagerness to excel and have a greater credit appetite to realize their dreams. Some of the needs include higher education and renting homes.

As such, most prefer credit solutions to create assets over time. At the same time, they also seek wealth protection and insurance schemes.

The conventional wisdom holds that individuals in their 20s and 30s can embark on risk since they have a lot of time to handle and address the inevitable rough patches. As such, many financial experts suggest all-stock portfolios for these individuals. However, not every young investor can handle the markets. For instance, many millennials are particularly wary in terms of stocks. Hence, young investors should get into stocks and take early risks. Nervous investors in this demographic should embark on a 60% stock allocation with the remainder in bonds, and maintain this combination throughout the market cycle. The primary goal is for young investors to experience the euphoria of bull markets and the desolation of bear markets.

Middle-aged individuals comprise those with nearly a decade of work experience. This demographic seeks to invest maximum and channel more money for family and lifestyle expenses. They establish assets with a combination of credit and investment avenues. In short, they have a diversified portfolio. Some of the typical expenses include purchasing a house and planning for retirement. Here, credit can play a vital part in meeting some of the essential expenses for this segment. It enables them to set aside some funds each month through instalments to realize their aspirations and save for early retirement. In addition, the protection of wealth continues to be the main focus for protecting financial status and setting aside an emergency fund.

Individuals in their 40s and 50s are probably hitting their peak earning years. Similarly, their financial expenses are also at peak, such as college tuition. Some investors are comfortable with more equities, but others prefer the extra stability offered by bonds. For those who have excellent saving habits, investing in low-risk ventures is the best approach. Nonetheless, individuals who wait until they reach their 40s have to increase their risk levels. Financial experts recommend a portfolio of 60% in stocks and 40% in bonds. However, given the current near record-low interest rates, an investor should embark on shorter maturities for bonds and invest in high-yield bonds since they are less sensitive to rate hikes. Furthermore, assets allocation changes over time, hence, this demographic should look for areas that are undervalued and allocate more there.

The senior individuals segment comprises a class of professionals that is wiser, experience, and approaching retirement. These people have a low risk-taking appetite and are focused on wealth protection. Although their involvement in credit reduces, they have a succession plan in place. Here, a comprehensive investment plan will allow them to reinvest in investment returns to increase their retirement funds. With retirement on the horizon when one is in their 60s, an individual may be imagining what it might look like for them, researching the options, and getting serious about laying the groundwork for this next chapter of life. Here, financial experts recommend a 60/40 portfolio of stocks and bonds. However, individuals playing catch-up should lean more on stocks to power their savings. At the same time, individuals need to balance their need for growth and stability. A portfolio that declines early in retirement can be devastating in the future because of withdrawals. Here, experts suggest combining your equity stake with a home-equity line of credit that can be used for cash requirements if the portfolio is down temporarily.

In your 70s, you may be retired and adjusting to a new normal with a hobby or spending time with grandchildren. Some people find it difficult to change from an "accumulating assets" mindset to spending their retirement funds. On the other hand, it is tempting to think that your asset-allocations decisions are done now that you have retired. However, the need for growth is crucial even in retirement. Your portfolio has to last until you are dead, probably three decades. Hence, one requires stability. You can evenly split the portfolio between stocks and bonds. In addition, financial gurus suggest a bucker approach. Here, you set aside a few years of required income in temporary bonds to cover your expenses. The rest can be invested for growth and you can replenish the expenses bucket when the markets are performing well. When the markers are down, you have enough money to weather the storm.

ii.   What's Your Personal Outlook for Next 5/10 Years?

It is conventional wisdom that younger individuals have a long-term time horizon when planning on investment and taking more risks. When it comes to how much one risks to take, one must consider the investment. When will the funds be required? If the time horizon is fairly short, risk-taking should move to become more conservative. On the other hand, for long-term investments, there is adequate space for aggressive investing. However, one should be careful when adhering to conventional wisdom in terms of risk tolerance. With life expectancies and advancing medical science, a 60-year-old individual may still have a 22-year-old time horizon.

Moreover, net worth and available capital must be taken into consideration when determining the amount of risk to take. Your net worth is the assets you have minus liabilities. Risk capital is the funds available for investment or trade that will not impact your lifestyle when lost. Individuals with high net worth can embark on more risk. Unfortunately, investors with little or no net worth and restricted risk capital are frequently drawn to riskier investments, such as options, because of the appeal of quick, easy, and huge returns. Another thing to consider while taking risk is calculating how much risk can be tolerated. Here, just because an individual can embark on riskier investments does not mean that they should. For instance, if capital preservation is the aim and you are a new investor, be cautious of undertaking too much risk. In addition, your level of investment experience plays a major role in your investment endeavors. It is crucial to commence new ventures with caution and gather experience before committing too much money.

You should undertake a risk that is appropriate to your situation so that when the worst-case scenario occurs, you can fight another day. Finally, careful consideration of the risk is vital when making investment decisions. Here, spreading your risk reduces your overall exposure to any single investment. With correct diversification, the likelihood of total loss is significantly minimized. However, understanding one's risk tolerance is a sophisticated process that involves striking a balance between the financial situation and goals.

The Importance of Portfolio Construction

Portfolio construction is all about investing in a range of funds that combine to create an investment solution for investors. Creating a portfolio encompasses comprehending various kinds of investment and combining them to fulfill set investment goals and objectives. The portfolio construction involves comprehension of needs and goals and matching an investment approach with the specific circumstances to reduce the overall investment risk. There are four primary aims of portfolio construction which include: controlling risk, matching an investment approach with needs and objectives, aids create a level of expectation for portfolio performance from the selected investment strategy, and guiding the expected volatility linked with the investment approach.

A good portfolio should contain multiple objectives and realize a sound balance among them. First, one needs to have a stable current return. Once investment security is assured, the portfolio should generate a stable current income. The current yields should at least equal the opportunity cost of the funds invested. Second, we have marketability. An excellent portfolio encompasses investments that can easily be marketed. When there are numerous inactive shares in the portfolio, one may encounter hurdles in disposing of them or moving from one investment to another. It is advisable to invest in firms whose shares are actively traded. Third, since a tax regulation is a fundamental element in planning, an effective portfolio must consider income tax, capital gains, tax, and gift tax during its construction. As a result, it will help you in tax planning. Four, a good portfolio should appreciate safeguarding the investor from losing their buying power because of inflation. Here, a balanced portfolio should have specific investments that appreciate real value after altering for inflation. In addition, a portfolio guarantees that there is adequate money on short notice for the investor to cater to liquidity needs. Hence, it is advisable to have a line of credit from the bank for use in case of an emergency. Finally, a portfolio guarantees that your investment is secure (*Invest blue*).

i.　Diversification and Stability

Recall when you played hide and seek as a child? The ideal approach was for everyone to hide in different locations within the house. As a result, even if one or two kids lost, the rest has the chance to win the game. This is what diversification entails. Portfolio diversification is the act of investing funds in varying assets and securities to reduce the overall risk. Imagine what would happen if you put all your funds in a single asset. Things would be good as long as the asset performed well. However, in case of a sudden market crash, you would lose your entire savings in a single moment. This is what occurs when all the children in the hide and seek game hide in the same place. When the seeker finds them, everyone loses and the game ends.

Diversification is the technique of spreading your investments in a way that your exposure to any kind of asset is limited. This approach is intended to help minimize the volatility of the portfolio with time and to maximize returns by investing in varying areas that react differently. The key to successful investing is learning how to balance your investment against your time horizon. Invest in your retirement conservatively at a young age, and you will run the danger of having an investment growth rate that cannot keep pace with inflation (Fabozzi & Markowitz, 2011). On the other hand, if you invest aggressively in the later stages of your life, you can leave your savings unprotected from market unpredictability, which can reduce the value of your investments at a period where you have fewer chances to recover your losses.

One of the primary ways to balance risk and rewards in your portfolio is through diversification. It can help lessen the risk and volatility in your portfolio, possibly minimizing the effects of unpredictability. Most financial experts agree that, although diversification does not protect from loss, it is the most essential aspect of realizing long-term financial goals while minimizing risks. How does diversification work? Imagine you have a portfolio that only comprises airline stocks. Here, share prices may decline after a bad incident, such as an unspecified pilot strike that might lead to the cancelation of flights. As a result, your portfolio will undergo a significant drop in value. Here, you can counterbalance the airline stocks with some railway stocks, meaning that only a section of your portfolio will be impacted. There is also a high chance that the railway stocks will increase in value since more passengers will be seeking substitute means of transportation. In addition, you could diversify to other ventures due to the dangers linked with these firms. Anything that impacts travel with damage both sectors since air and railway stocks exhibit a strong correlation. Therefore, you should diversify your portfolio across varying industries and organizations. The more uncorrelated investments you have, the better.

Diversification helps reduced exposure to risk, which improves the stability and potential yields of an investment portfolio. It helps investors to create a strong portfolio. Although some may prefer higher risk for greater returns, most investors want a stable and reliable way to secure their financial goals. It is essential to have clear investment goals since an individual who is saving for retirement may have a completely different risk tolerance and time horizon than an individual investing for short-term goals.

Since risk mitigation is the primary principle in portfolio diversification, it is fundamental to comprehend which types of risk diversification can minimize, and how a decline in those risks can affect a portfolio's efficiency. Unsystematic risk, also called diversifiable risk is a portfolio risk distinct to an asset class (*Invest blue*). It comprises dangers that are distinct to a firm, industry, market or other segments within the financial system (Fabozzi & Markowitz, 2011). The vulnerability emanating from unsystematic risk can be reduced via a portfolio management approach that diversifies investments across financial markets that do not share identical unsystematic risks. Consequently, creating a diversified investment portfolio with little or no correlation can mitigate the effect of any losses from a specific firm, asset class, sector, or region.

Systematic risk is the risk intrinsic to the financial structure as a whole. It includes trends that affect the entire global financial system, like rising inflation and interest rates. Although it is impossible to eradicate exposure to the danger of an economic downturn, it is possible to diversify into ventures that minimize the loss in case of such events, particularly in the long run. For instance, when interest rates rise, purchasing fixed-income assets with the capacity of realizing high returns, like bonds, could offset losses. Furthermore, putting your money on hard assets, like commercial real estate, can help protect against inflation increases and lead to better long-term yields.

Moreover, diversification leads to lower risk and higher portfolio return potential. When the risk is correctly lessened via diversification, it is less susceptible to volatility. The portfolio is more stable, and its yield potential is more anticipated. Although diversification cannot do away with risk, a well-structured diversified portfolio can lead to improved risk-adjusted earnings. Financial experts use mean-variance analysis to calculate a portfolio's risk. In addition, the effect of diversification is visible in the long-term time horizon and monetary objectives. For instance, if you are saving for retirement with an account, an efficient diversification approach will demonstrate its value over the years.

How do you diversify your portfolio? Diversification is the primary doctrine of investing since it facilitates better risk management. Nonetheless, one needs to approach it with caution. One should spread out their investment portfolio. Investing in equities is an excellent move but one does not have to put all their money on a single stock or industry. This also applies to other investments including mutual funds, precious metals, and fixed deposits. For example, you could invest in six stocks (Fabozzi & Markowitz, 2011). However, if the entire market suddenly crashes, you might have a problem, which is escalated if the stocks are in the same industry, such as hospitality. This shows that even if you select the same asset, you should diversify by venturing into varying sectors and companies. There is an unlimited number of industries and companies to invest in including, mining, energy, pharmaceuticals, and many more.

Furthermore, you can explore other investment avenues for your portfolio. Here, you can consider bonds, real estate, mutual funds, and pension initiatives. Similarly, ensure that the securities of these ventures have different risks and adhere to varying markers forces. Generally, bonds and equity markers have opposing movements. Hence, by venturing into both markets, you can counterbalance any harmful results in one market to make sure you do not enter a lose-lose situation. In addition, adding bond funds to the portfolio can provide much-required stability. At the same time, investing in Index funds is a highly cost-effective strategy since its charge are relatively low compared to actively managed funds (Guerard Jr, 2009). Similarly, putting money in bond funds safeguards the portfolio from markets unpredictability and prevents gains from being reduced to zero during markets volatility.

Another portfolio diversification approach is to keep building your portfolio. It is important to continue creating your portfolio by investing in varying asset classes, spreading across equities, debt, and fixed-return tools. Implementing this strategy can allow you to better mitigate volatility and remain invested across market cycles (Guerard Jr, 2009). In addition, portfolio diversification involves knowing when to exit your investments. If the asset category you have been investing in has not performed as expected for a long time, you must exit. This is the same for any fundamental changes to the portfolio that do not align with your goals and risk appetite. Similarly, it is vital to note that those invested in any market-linked tool should not exit after short-term unpredictability. Another vital factor to consider is commissions. For those using the investment services of a professional, they must check out the fees they are incurring. This helps to prevent commissions from taking a toll on the end yields.

There are four main components of a diversified portfolio: domestic stocks, bonds, short-term investments, and international stocks. Stocks are the most aggressive part of the portfolio and offer the chance for greater growth in the long run. Nonetheless, the higher probability for growth carries a greater risk, especially in the short term. This is because stocks are typically more volatile than other kinds of assets. International stocks are issued by international companies and often perform differently than domestic firms, offering exposure to opportunities not provided by US securities. Those looking for investments with greater potential yields and higher risks should add foreign stocks to their portfolios.

Most bonds offer consistent interest income and are typically regarded as less unpredictable than stocks. Bonds can also serve as cushions against volatility since they behave differently from stocks. Investors who prefer safety to growth favor bonds, while minimizing their exposure to stocks. These individuals understand that bonds offer lower returns than stocks in the long term. Nonetheless, some fixed-income investments, such as high-yield bonds and specific global bonds, can provide greater returns, accompanied by more risk. On the other hand, short-term investments include money funds and short-term CDs (certificates of deposit) (Guerard Jr, 2009). Money market funds are perfect for those seeking to preserve principal since they are conservative ventures that provide stability and easy access to funds. In return for safety, money markers typically offer lower yields than bonds. Although money markets are seen as secure, they are not insured by the Deposit Insurance Corporation how CDs are protected.

Sector stocks concentrate on a specific section of the economy. They can be vital instruments for investors looking for opportunities in varying stages of the economic cycle. Although only then most knowledgeable investors should save on commodities, adding equity funds that concentrate on commodity-intensive sectors to your portfolio, like mining and gas, can offer a hedge against inflation. In addition, real estate funds can play a part in portfolio diversification and offer some safeguards against inflation. For individuals who lack the time or knowledge to create a diversified portfolio, asset allocation funds can act as an effective single-fund approach.

How does diversification help minimize the impact of market volatility? The main purpose of diversification is not to maximize yields, but to lessen the effect of volatility on a portfolio. To understand the concept of diversification, let us look at chart 5 below, which illustrates hypothetical portfolios with varying asset allocations.

If there was a period that illustrates the effectiveness of creating a diversified portfolio, it would be now. Since the start of the Covid-19 pandemic, stock prices have been all over the place, as investors unsuccessfully react to the effect of the global health pandemic on the global economy and the stock markets. It is unsuccessful since it is an evolving scenario and the extent of its effect on stability is still uncertain. Although the effect is not easily measurable, the economy is facing a recession. To support businesses during these uncertain times, various Central Banks around the planet have reduced interest rates. As a result, bond prices have increased. Currently, although equity prices have gone down, bond prices keep on going up. Today, investors with well-diversified portfolios that are spread across equity and fixed income tools are likely to come out fairly unscratched from the existing turmoil. This illustrates the significance of portfolio diversification.

ii.   Emotions in Investing

It is a sad fact, but close to 40% of individuals that win the lottery go into bankruptcy within five years. Contrary to what we know, economic recessions and anticipated personal crises are never a factor. Lottery winners on average lack the adequate emotional intelligence to sensibly manage their money (Gutkevych & Vikhliaiev, 2021). Emotions play a vital role in investing. Emotional intelligence (EQ) entails comprehending your capacity to discriminate between emotions and rational decision-making. It is about understanding your inner belief system and creating a successful relationship between you and your money. Reflect on your character and its impact on your relationship with cash. Are you a conservative individual who misses put on higher yields because of adversity to risk? No matter who you are, your personality has a profound impact on how you approach money, investments, and your portfolio. Based on your personality, your relationship will vary dramatically.

Based on your emotional personality, you will approach investing differently from an individual with a different character. Generosity and aggressiveness play a huge part in how you manage your money. A generous individual will allocate more resources in their portfolio towards socially conscious investments. On the downside, such a person may have a hard time saying no to requests of cash from family members, negatively affecting their portfolio performance. Hence, understanding your emotional personality is crucial for self-awareness and the key to establishing a constructive relationship with your finances. In addition, your emotional personality plays a vital role when it comes to dealing with externalities. No portfolio is immune to unanticipated externalities, such as recessions, stock crashes, or unexpected health expenses. Wealth accumulation is typically a boring process that emanates from deliberate steps. Only a handful of individuals become rich from hair-triggered, emotional decisions. Therefore, comprehending your personality is essential to correctly manage external situations. The other option is to fall victim to hot-headed emotions, which generally leads to disposing of or purchasing at a bad time.

The two most prevalent strategies to investing are dollar-cost averaging and diversification. These strategies allow investors to eliminate the guesswork in investment decisions and minimize the danger of poor timing because of emotional investing. The most effective approach of the two is the dollar-cost averaging. This is an approach where an equal amount of dollars is invested at an ordered, predetermined interval. It can be used in any market situation. In a downward trending market, investors buy shares at reduced prices. On the other hand, during an upward trend, the shares held in the portfolio are generating capital gains. Similarly, since the dollar investment is a static amount, fewer shares are bought when the share price is higher. The most essential aspect of the dollar-cost averaging approach is to stay on course. Here, you should formulate a strategy and do not interfere with it unless a major alteration mandates re-examination and reorganization of the original course. This approach is more effective in plans with matching benefits since a static dollar amount is deducted from the salary and the employer offers extra contributions.

How to Construct a Portfolio

Most of the investment advice focuses on generating as much yields as possible for the least amount of time. What about accepting the probability of risk and actively looking to establish a high-risk investment portfolio? Such a portfolio may contain significant prospects for higher returns, but investors must have the proper knowledge when approaching this type of investment.

i.   **High Risk Portfolio**

The best way to think about risk is in terms of the probability of an investment either underperforming or leading in a considerable loss of capital. A high-risk investment is where the chances of underperformance, or losing all the investment, are greater than average (Hunjra, 2020). These investment ventures provide investors the prospect for bigger yield for accepting the associated degree of risk. Many high-risk ventures are categorized as alternative investments and are utilized to balance a portfolio and introduce investment opportunities that have little or no market correlation.

We can never stipulate that there is a direct relationship between risk and reward since some risks may not have any reward. We can only say that there is a positive relationship between risk and potential reward. Hence, investors after huge returns in relatively short time must accept a disproportional higher degree of risk. In addition, the connection between risk and reward is not always predictable, but there is a time-tested correlation between the two concepts. If investors wish for greater returns, they must accept to undertake more risk (Russo, 2013). Hence, if an investor is willing to accept higher risk, they have a probability of realizing significantly higher returns. However, numerous investors fall victim to false superiority and optimism bias. These two cognitive preconceptions conglomerate to make us believe that we will thrive where others have failed.

Not all risk is harmful for the individual investor. The best approach is accepting the proper risk. There are varying notions of risks. Keeping an all-cash portfolio is risky since the value of money can be eroded by inflation. In addition, large institutions cannot afford the risks associated with low liquidity, but that threshold is inferior for an individual. Another primary element of high-risk portfolios is volatility (Royal, 2021). Although numerous financial experts and market participants do not utilize volatility as a substitution for risk, volatility is a poor equivalence of risk. For investors, risk is the probability of loss from an investment. Some stocks experience considerable swings but also generate significant returns for investors.

A fundamental aspect to note when creating a high-risk portfolio is that not all risk is the same. This means that investors should only pursue smart risks, which they get rewarded for taking. For example, investing in the shares of bankrupt businesses is always a bad option. Even if the business survives, the bankruptcy process almost wipes out equity for investors and no sufficient room to validate the risk. In addition, investor must guard against idleness and complacency. High-risks investing mandates awareness and attention to detail. Hence, creating a portfolio without thorough due diligence and overlooking it is high-risk investing that will not get you extra rewards. Furthermore, investors must be smart about leverage. It is appropriate to utilize leverage to increase potential returns in a portfolio, but investors must be vigilant to restrict their maximum losses to a degree that they can tolerate.

There are various types of high-risk portfolios. You can build a high-risk portfolio without altering investment strategies. Investing heavily in a single industry can definitely increase risk and potential yield. For example, investors who invested heavily in technology stocks in the later 1990s got handsome returns as well as those who effectively participate in cyclical commodity runs. Concentrating on a single sector is an approach that grounded on a good understanding of the industry.

Similarly, it is vital to comprehend the market psychology and moods and concentrating on an unpopular industry is likely not to ramp up yields.

Another high-risk investing strategy for your portfolio is momentum investing. The concept behind momentum investing is to put your money in stocks that are displaying strong price action. The risk associated with this strategy is linked to the above-average valuations that famous stocks carry, but costly stocks can frequently trade up before fading. Momentum investing mandates a sturdy selling self-restraint. Here, investors can seek to a diversified portfolio that to reduce absolute risk, but a comprehensive market decline hit the growth of the portfolio hard unless the investor is flexible enough to go short.

There are many financial experts and information websites that discourage investors from undertaking penny stocks, stressing on the frequency of deception, corruption, and illiquidity of these stocks. Although these are valid concerns, the huge risks associated with these stocks do payoff. Investing in penny stocks mandates extraordinary dedication to due diligence, and diversification can aid minimize risk.

Additionally, high-risk investors should seek to invest in emerging technology companies. Such ventures provide investors with opportunities in new technologies and commodities (Russo, 2013). In this strategy, diversification is vital, since investors must be patient and ready to endure low batting average since most emerging technology companies fail. Therefore, investors must concentrate on firms that contain capital or access to capital.

Moreover, futures and options offer leverage since a handful amount of capital can control a large amount of capital. Currency and futures transactions mandate a unique combination of patience, confidence, and agility. Futures are different from stocks because an investor has to make the right decision, but the expected move has to occur before the contract expires. On the other hand, options and option approaches control the range, for low-risk yield creating approaches to extremely high-risk approaches that can have huge returns under fairly restricted conditions. Another high-risk investment is cryptocurrencies. These are digital currencies that operate independently from central banks. Although there are investors who have made huge returns from markets, they are extremely volatile and many have lost considerable

funds. In addition, high risk investors can seek angel investing. An

ideal high-risk portfolio should comprise of 50% Speculative, 10%

Cash, 30% Income (Dividend/Real Estate), and 10% Gold/Bonds as

shown in figure 5.

Figure 5: *Example of a High-risk Portfolio*

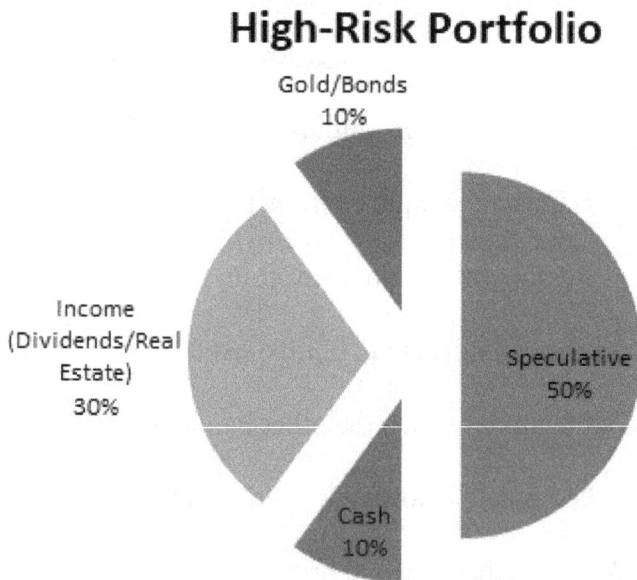

High-Risk Portfolio

Gold/Bonds
10%

Income
(Dividends/Real
Estate)
30%

Speculative
50%

Cash
10%

Investors with the monetary ability to tolerate risk should do so.

With time, intelligence and discipline can generate considerable above-average yields. The vital aspect is that investors must undertake risks that can yield better returns and firmly avoid risks that do not lead to addition funds to their portfolio.

ii.   Mid Risk Portfolio

A mid risk portfolio is also known as a moderate portfolio where the investor wants to protect most of the portfolio's value but is ready to tolerate some risk for inflation. It is a portfolio where an investor has a medium risk tolerance and a time limit longer than five years. Investors are ready to endure some market volatility in exchange for yields that surpass inflation. A standard mid-risk portfolio includes 20% speculative assets, 20% cash, 50% income, and 10% gold or bonds as depicted in figure 6. A general approach within this portfolio structure is current income. Here, you select securities that pay a higher degree of dividends. One can choose to invest 40% in large-cap stocks, 10% in small-cap stock, 15% in foreign stock fund, 30% in intermediate-term bonds, and 5% in money market fund. From this portfolio, an investor can get an average yearly return of 7-8%, with its best annual yield being around 20-30%, and its largest annual decline ranging from 20-25%. The majority of investors fall into the low-risk

investment category.

Figure 6: *Example of a Mid-risk Portfolio*

Mid-Risk Portfolio

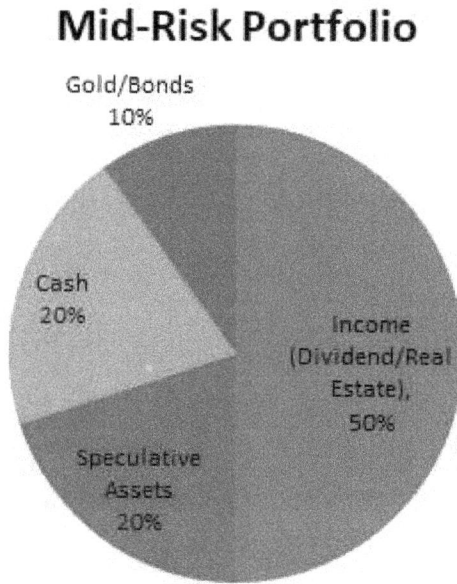

Gold/Bonds
10%

Cash
20%

Income
(Dividend/Real
Estate),
50%

Speculative
Assets
20%

Swensen developed a portfolio allocation model for individual

investors, which created a 20% rule. The rule stipulates that you should

diversify at least 20% of their investment portfolio into alternatives, like

real estate. As a way of balancing portfolio risk and individual risk

tolerance with optimal potential yields, Swensen suggested a portfolio

structure that comprise of 20% allocation to alternative assets and 80%

allocation to a wide range of traditional assets (Russo, 2013). In this framework, allocating a huge percentage of a portfolio to an alternative asset class that offers constructive diversification. The lowers the risk volatility and ultimate loss. In addition, some scholars agree that an investment portfolio with a 20% allocation to alternative investment has performed better than those invested only in traditional investments. Although numerous institutional investors, including endowments and pensions, put 20% or more into alternatives, single investors are not as diversified.

A primary feature of the 20% rule is that is recommends investing in alternative asset classes, which are traded in the private market, as opposed to stocks and bonds in the public market. The difference in markets is a primary reason why alternative assets have little or no correlation with traditional assets. The primary market operates under different dynamics than the public market. Although the public market is very efficient, the private market is inefficient because of several reasons, including friction, information asymmetry, and fragmentation.

iii.   Low Risk Portfolio

A low-risk portfolio is a known as conservative portfolio and its primary aim is to protect the principal value of a portfolio. A low-risk strategy typically allocates a huge portion of the funds to lower-risk securities, like money market and fixed income securities. Regardless of whether you are extremely conservative and seek to avoid the stock market completely, some exposure to stocks can help counterbalance inflation. Hence, one can invest the equity percentage in technology companies or an index fund. For low-risk portfolio investors, an extended time horizon is important. This is because conservative investors are not ready to tolerate periods of extreme market volatility and look for returns that match or surpass inflation (Royal, 2021). An ideal low risk portfolio should comprise of 5% speculative assets, 30% cash, 50% income, and 15% gold or bonds as illustrated in figure 7.

Figure 7: *Example of a Low-risk Portfolio*

Low-Risk Portfolio

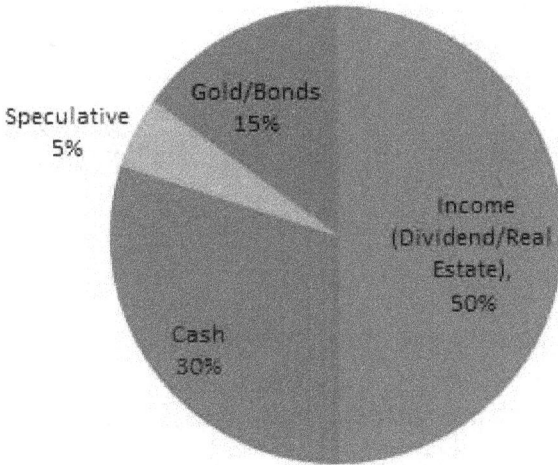

Although not technically an investment, savings accounts

provide modest return on your money. A savings account is entirely

safe and most accounts are government-insured, meaning one will be

compensated if the financial institution fails. The only drawback of a

saving account is that inflation can erode the purchasing power of money. Certificates of deposit (CDs) offer low-risk investment since they are loss-proof in a government-backed account. Certificates of deposits are ideal for conservative investors because when you leave them untouched until they expire, the bank pledges to pay you a set of rate of interest over the specified term. However, if you remove money from CDs early, you will lose some of the interested earned. Similarly, some banks will also hit you with a loss of a portion of principal as well. Furthermore, money market funds offer liquidity and are relatively safe. Investors could also invest in corporate bonds, such as high-yield bonds.

These portfolio models and strategies only provide a standard guideline. You can alter the proportions to fit your investment goals. The appropriate approach depends on what type of an investor you are and your financial requirements. For example, if you perform individual research on your companies and dedicate time to stock selection, you will likely divide your equities portion into subclasses. This will allow you to realize a specialized risk-yield potential within a percentage of your portfolio. At the same time, the proportion of the portfolio dedicated to money market tools will rely on the amount of liquidity and protection you require (Hunjra, 2020). Hence, if you require in investments that you can liquidate swiftly, you can consider placing a bigger percentage of the portfolio in money markets or temporary fixed-income securities. On the other hand, investors who do not prefer liquidity and have greater risk endurance will have a tiny percentage of their portfolio within these tools.

As you construct your portfolio, you might select one of the many basic allocation strategies. Each approach provides varying benefits grounded on the investor's time limit, objectives, and risk endurance (Royal, 2021). Hence, when the portfolio is active, it is crucial to perform a periodic review. This entails a consideration of your life goals and financial goals. Irrespective of fixed priorities, your portfolio mandates rebalancing.

Asset allocation is a vital investing principle that allows investors to maximize returns while minimizing risk. The varying asset allocation approaches discussed above cover many investment methods, accommodating different risk endurance, time frames, and objectives

(Hunjra, 2020). Therefore, when selecting an asset allocation strategy that fit your needs, remember to reexamine your portfolio periodically to make sure that you are preserving your planned allocation and are still on track for your long-tern financial goals.

Speculative Assets

The main part of investing advice, particularly for individuals interested in retirement facilities, revolves around slow and consistent gains over decades. However, not every investor is happy with the prospect of patient long-term returns. For some, home run trade is better since it is a move that can alter their fortunes overnight. This is called speculation and it comes with considerable risk. Speculation is the act of purchasing or selling assets that have an increased probability of considerable losses. Speculative investors take more risk with the anticipation of extraordinary returns which acts as compensation for the huge risk. Most of these investors are active traders; they seek to beat the market average and have a better hand-on strategy, particularly during temporary swings in the market. This is opposite to more passive, purchase-and-hold investors who normally apply a hand-off strategy and do not alter their portfolios regularly.

An investor who buys a speculative asset is likely concentrated on price fluctuations.

Although the risk linked with the asset is high, speculators are normally concerned with generating a profit grounded on market value changes for that asset rather than long-term investing. Although speculative investing encompasses the purchase of a foreign currency, it is called currency speculation. In such a situation, a speculator purchases a currency seeking to sell it later when it appreciates. Without the probability of considerable returns, there would be little incentive to participate in speculation.

The decision-making process for speculative investors differs extensively in terms of complexity. For some, investment decisions are made grounded on social media groups and memes. This was the main force behind the surge in stock prices for firms such as GameStop and AMC Theaters. Another example is Dogecoin, a cryptocurrency that experienced enormous spikes at the start of 2021 when famous personalities, such as Elon Musk, discussed it on Twitter. After Elon Musk's appearance on Saturday Night Live, Dogecoin fell more than 30% (Philavong & Phomvongsa, 2021). In addition, a sequence of tweets from Musk was to blame for the volatility of Bitcoin after Tesla stated that it would not accept Bitcoin as a form of payment. In April

2021, the price of Bitcoin was around $65,300, but it fell to $33,000 after Tesla`s announcement (Philavong & Phomvongsa, 2021). On the other hand, some speculators base their decisions on a hunch or market volatility. These investors look for information that demonstrates the potential to them and risks to other individuals. Almost all markets have a speculative corner.

Speculation works when investors have a strong understanding or perspective about an industry. Next, they generally identify a facilitator or event likely to trigger a considerable movement toward their original prediction. When an investor feels that the event is probable, they will purchase assets they believe will gather most returns once their prediction occurs. A primary example is the 2020 election cycle. At the time, the majority believed that if Joe Biden won the presidency, that cannabis would be legalized by the national government. As a result, firms, such as Tilray (TLRY) and Aurora Cannabis, were ground zero for speculators (Apergis, Hayat & Saeed, 2021). Speculation is common among penny stocks and over-the-counter investments. Firms that deal in the OTC markets are not informal exchanges, like the NASDAQ. Hence, they are inexpensive but are highly risky since they lack oversight and have a shaky monetary history.

For instance, real estate can blur the line between investment and speculation when purchasing property to rent it out. Although this can be termed as investing, purchasing many properties with minimal down payments for the aim of reselling swiftly at a profit is regarded as speculation. Hence, speculators can facilitate market liquidity and constrict the bid-ask spread, allowing producers to hedge price risk competently. In addition, speculative short-selling can keep rampant bullishness in check and prevent the creation of asset price bubbles via hedging against successful results. Mutual and hedge funds frequently participate in speculation in the foreign exchange, bonds, and stock markets.

Foreign exchange is a highly speculative market where investors trade currencies, such as the Japanese Yen and the British Pound, without a centralized exchange. The primary purpose of these markets is to take advantage of short-term price fluctuations between currencies. Foreign markets have the planet's highest total volume and dollar value, with an estimated $6.6 trillion exchanging hands per day (Apergis,

Hayat & Saeed, 2021). Foreign exchange markets trade across the globe while positions can be taken and reversed in seconds, using instant electronic trading platforms. Transactions in these markets generally feature spot deals to purchase and sell currency pairs. The market is dominated by asset managers and hedge funds with portfolios worth billions of dollars. However, speculation in foreign exchange markets can be difficult to differentiate from normal hedging actions, which take place when a firm purchases or sell a currency to hedge against markets cycles. For instance, a sale of foreign currency associated with a bond purchase can be seen as a hedge of the bond's value or normal speculation.

The universal bond market is worth over $100 trillion. Bonds are issued by governments and multinational companies. Asset prices can vary hugely and are strongly impacted by interest rate cycles and politics. The largest single market trades US Treasuries (Apergis, Hayat & Saeed, 2021). In some circles, the concepts of speculation and investment are utilized interchangeably. However, there is a huge difference between investing and speculating. Investors and traders make calculated risks as they seek to get returns from transactions they make in the markets. The degree of risk incurred in these transactions and the types of financial instruments used are the primary difference between investing and speculating. When an individual takes up an asset with the expectation of returning a profit, they are investing. Here, a reasonable judgment is made after an extensive analysis shows that the venture has a good probability of success. However, what if the same individual puts money in a venture that illustrates a high chance of failure? Here, they are speculating since success or failure relies mainly on probability or uncontrollable factors. Hence, the key difference between investing and speculating is the degree of risk undertaken. High-risk speculation is linked to gambling, while lower-risk investing utilizes a basis of fundamentals and analysis.

The word `speculative` has a negative connotation to it, like the asset in question is in a bubble and the spectator is not well informed. However, a speculative asset does not produce earnings, interest, rent, or income. It includes assets such as gold, land, cryptocurrency. Speculative assets are difficult to value at any given time because there are no future returns to utilize to determine their value. Naturally, every asset has some speculative aspects, but they typically make up only a small part of the return of the asset in the long term. When we have a speculative asset, the speculative element dominates the yields, even in the long run.

Speculative stocks are clustered in industries, such as mining, energy, technology, and biotechnology. Although there is significant risk involved in investing in the early-stage firms in these industries, the probability that a small company will find a colossal mineral deposit, invent a popular app, or discover a cure for an illness provides adequate motivation for speculators to invest in them (Apergis, Hayat & Saeed, 2021). While most of the speculative stocks occur in early-stage firms, a blue-chip can occasionally become a speculative stock if it encounters challenging events that reduce its prospects. Such a stock is called a fallen angel.

One of the most common speculative assets is gold. This precious metal has a long history in the world economy. Human beings have been using gold as an investment, currency, or store of value for centuries. There is a limited amount of gold in the world and new gold is hard to find or mine (Hillier, Draper & Faff, 2006). Gold does not expire or lust, making it a durable commodity and store of value.

Although gold can be volatile, its long-term returns are famous since it has proven that it can keep up with inflation over the centuries. It is a perfect speculative asset for investors who like to hedge against precious metals. The only disadvantage with gold is that it must be stored, protected, and insured. Furthermore, silver is a good speculative asset. Silver has fewer returns than gold with more volatility. The primary advantage of silver is that it does have many industrial uses.

Another speculative asset is cryptocurrency. The best aspect of cryptocurrency investment is that your yields may be incredible. As technology advances, cryptocurrency has become a major way of transacting and storing value. Currently, there are many cryptocurrencies throughout the world but the most famous include Bitcoin, Etherum, and Dogecoin (Philavong & Phomvongsa, 2021). Although cryptocurrency is not centralized or controlled by governments, it has become a primary investment venture for most people because of its capabilities. It gives an individual autonomy and cuts out the middle man in most transactions. If the cryptocurrency you invest in becomes the de facto currency in the future and you got to have it before it becomes prevalent, you can become a millionaire with a small investment that cannot impact your financial goals at the moment. This is what happened to Bitcoin in the last few years. Developed at the start of the last decade, the value of Bitcoin skyrocketed as governments and businesses started using cryptocurrency to trade. Consequently, this lottery element has inspired many individuals to add cryptocurrency to their portfolios.

Hence, cryptocurrency should be part of your portfolio. One of the advantages of cryptocurrency is that they are easy to conceal and transport. In addition, they are not insured and are taxed at capital gains rates. However, there are several drawbacks to having cryptocurrency as an investment. It can be lost and new ones are invented at any time. Furthermore, cryptocurrency is extremely volatile, which means that its future returns could be severe. Hence, we should look for ones that can stand the test of time and that increase in value with time.

Moreover, high-end art falls in the speculative asset category. Art is a favored speculative asset, especially for the wealthy. The most expensive art tends to appreciate at a higher rate than normal art since the returns often range between 5.3% and 7.5%. A speculator can purchase the art at an auction or purchase it via a private art fund.

Although most people derive pleasure from observing and showing off their art, most high-end art is not displayed to the public. It is stored in a secure facility. However, the drawbacks of art as a speculative asset are the costs of storage and insurance.

The speculative portfolio is close to gambling as it involves taking more risk. Speculative moves include initial public offerings (IPOs) or stocks that are alleged to be annexation targets. Hence, technology or biotechnology companies on the verge of creating a single breakthrough product fall in this category. For example, a young oil firm about to release its first production outcomes would be a speculative move for investors. Here, financial experts recommend that an individual's portfolio should contain no more than 10% in speculative assets. Today, the leveraged exchange-traded funds represent speculation. These are investments that are attractive since choosing one can lead to colossal profits in a short among of time. Hence, the speculative portfolio mandates extensive research for it to be successful. In addition, it is also time-consuming.

Speculation is not for the faint-hearted. Although the allure for huge profits exists, it is wise to seek advice from a financial expert to ensure that you are not taking more than you can handle. In addition, consider undertaking an extensive risk assessment to allow you to prepare and comprehend how you will respond to losses. Finally, ensure that you have an existing plan to handle your immediate, short-term, and long-term monetary objectives and separate them from any speculative moves you want to undertake. If you decide to hedge your portfolio utilizing speculative assets, restrict how much you invest in. Although 1% is regarded as a small investment rather than a hedge, spending 5-10% of your portfolio on assets that do not generate profit, interest, or rent can have you working longer than you want to while having to manage a more sophisticated and costly portfolio along the way.

How to value Companies

Determining the fair value of a company can be a sophisticated task. After all, there are numerous factors to consider and it is an essential financial skill to comprehend. How do financial experts evaluate assets to establish a solid number? Business valuation is the process of assessing the total economic value of a business and its assets. During valuation, all elements of a business are assessed to determine its current worth. The evaluation encompasses gathering and assessing several aspects, such as revenue, profits, losses, risks, and opportunities a business encounter. It also entails examining a company`s management, its capital structure, and future earnings prospects. The purpose of business valuation is to calculate a business`s estimated intrinsic value and allow entrepreneurs and investors to make informed purchase, sale, or investment decisions (Vayas-Ortega et al., 2020). The tools utilized for valuation vary among financial experts, businesses, and industries. Valuation is also fundamental in tax reporting. Some tax-related activities like sale of shares will be tax depending on a company's valuation.

Nonetheless, the valuation process is not entirely scientific. There is a large amount of art involved since the monetary framework will depend on the subjective inputs. The estimates and assumptions made during the process makes valuation an educated guess at best. Valuations helps financial experts calculate the intrinsic value of an asset, which is often disconnected from its existing trading market price. Intrinsic value is objective and less impacted by temporary market cycles. The valuation process is intrinsically technical: the individual performing the assessment must have adequate financial knowledge. Hence, the evaluator must be conversant with the company's business model, its strategy, and have an extensive comprehension of the industry.

There are various factors to consider in the evaluation process. All considerations during evaluation fall into two categories: profitability and risk. This is because investors examine the opportunity cost of making the investment, and if a venture is profitable and induces less risk, it is more likely to be an investment option. Another factor to consider is personal reasons. Emotional and non-financial forces may influence the valuation process outcome. Therefore, it is fundamental to comprehend the primary reason for the trade for both parties of the transaction. Furthermore, the value of a company depends on external factors and market forces. Before conducting a valuation, the company`s past and present date must be accurate and correct. This will lead to a reliable estimation and valuable conclusions. The more comprehensive and detailed the information is about a business, the better quality and precision the results will be.

i.   Discounted Free Cash Flow method (DCF)

Discounted cash flow (DCF) is a valuation method utilized to estimate the value of an investment grounded on its anticipated future cash flows. It seeks to calculate the value of an investment today grounded on the predictions of future earnings. This method applies to the decisions of investors in companies or securities, like acquiring a firm, investing in a technology startup, or purchasing a stock.

Using DCF Method

There are several steps in the DCF method of valuation. First, take the average of the last three years free cash flow (FCF) of the firm. Then, multiply this FCF with the anticipated growth rate to estimate the FCF of the future. Next, calculate the net present value of this cash flow by dividing it by the discount factor. Repeat the same process for the next 10 years to find the net present value (NPV) of the future free cash flows. Add the NPV's of the FCF for all the ten years. After, find the terminal value the stock by multiplying the final year FCF with a terminal multiple factor. Finally, divide the calculated number in previous step by the total number of outstanding shares to arrive at the intrinsic value per share of the company.

For you to understand the DCF analysis, we must see how it is calculated. For instance, let's say we want to see if Apple stock was fairly valued at a specific point in time. On June 2008, Apple had a market capitalization of $150 billion. The firm was generating operating cash flow of close to $7 billion per year. We will assign a WACC of 7% to Apple since it is financially stable and can raise equity and debt capital economically. Similarly, we will assume that the company can expand its operating cash flow by 15% per annual in the next decade. From here, DCF would value Apple at a market cap of $106.3 billion, 30% below its stock market price at the time. Here, DCF offers an indication that the market may be paying too high for Apple's common stock.

The purpose of DCF is to estimate the funds an investor would get from an investment, adjusted for the time value of money. The value of money assumes that a dollar today is worth more than a dollar in the future since it can be invested. Hence, DCF assessment is suitable in any scenario where an individual is paying cash in the present with the anticipation of getting returns in the future. It identifies the present value of expected future cash flow utilizing a discount rate. Investors can utilize the notion of the present value of money to gauge if the future cash flows of an investment are identical or greater than the value of the initial investment (Vayas-Ortega et al., 2020). When the results of DCF are higher than the existing cost of investment, the opportunity cost should be taken into consideration. To perform a DCF assessment, investors must estimate future cash flows and the ending value of the asset. Then, the investor must also determine a suitable discount rate for the DCF framework, which vary depending on the investment. When the investors cannot access the relevant information or the investment is extremely sophisticated, DCF will not be efficient and substitute methods should be used.

The DCF method mandates analysis of past data to give an insight of the factors that lead to incurred cost and which generate revenues. Special attention should be given to the factors that might impact financial projections. In addition, market analysis and competitive must be considered during the evaluation. Comprehending the impacts of the Porter`s five forces will enable investors to predict future demand, measure the negotiation power of customers and suppliers, and understand a company`s vulnerability in the industry (Vayas-Ortega et al., 2020). Moreover, analyzing the competitors positioning in the industry will influence the value of the investment. After all the preliminary analyses are performed, the cash flow can be estimated. However, estimating accurate values is extremely sophisticated. Hence, buyers frequently calculate projections for a short time than sellers.

The primary drawback of DCF is that is mandates numerous assumptions. Hence, an investor must correctly estimate future cash flow from an investment. The future cash flow depends on various factors, like market demand, competition, technology, and unexpected risks and opportunities. In addition, estimating future cash flow incorrectly can result in selecting an investment that might not give returns in the future, affecting profits. Similarly, estimating cash flows to be too low can result in missed chances. Furthermore, selecting a discount rate for the framework is assumption and must be appropriate to make the model valuable.

ii.   Margin of Safety Method

Margin of safety is a standard of investing in which an investor only buys securities when their market value is considerably lower than their intrinsic value. When the market price of a security is considerably below your estimation of its intrinsic value, the difference is the margin safety. Since many investors may put a margin of safety based on their own risk preferences, purchasing securities when this variation exist enables an investment to be undertaken with negligible downside risk. The margin of safety became a popular valuation method because of the famous British-American investor Benjamin Graham and his followers (Battisti et al., 2019). Here, investors use both qualitative and quantitative factors, including company management, industry performance, and assets, to determine a security` intrinsic value. The mark up price is utilized as a point of comparison to calculate the margin of safety.

Calculating Margin of Safety

The formula for the margin of safety is:

Margin of Safety = 1 – Stock`s Current Price/Stock`s Intrinsic Value

First, we must calculate the intrinsic value and apply a margin of safety to the number to determine at what point we can buy. The formula for finding the value is;

$$V* = \frac{EPS \times (8.5 + 2g) \times 4.4}{Y}$$

Where:

IV = intrinsic value

EPS = Earnings per share

G = Expected growth rate

Y = current yield of 10 year Treasury notes

Let's say that we have Microsoft shares has the following

characteristics: Current EPS $2.09, Growth-7.05, and Yield at 2.14. The

intrinsic value is $43.11 and the current price of Microsoft shares is

$58.70. Here, Microsoft stocks are trading above the intrinsic value of

the company, which means you have no margin of safety if you buy at

its current price. To create a margin of safety you want to purchase it

below the intrinsic value. Hence, if you are looking for a 25% margin of

safety you would multiply the intrinsic value by 75%. In this case, it would mean $43.11 X 0.75 = $32.33. This is the price that you should look for as a buy.

Considering the margin of safety when investing offers a cushion against errors in calculations. Nonetheless, it does not guarantee a successful investment since determining a company's intrinsic value is extremely subjective. Despite the availability of varying methods for calculating intrinsic value, most of them are rarely accurate and precise. At the same time, it is particularly hard to predict a firm's future earnings.

A vital part of value investing is to make sure that there is a margin of safety with your investment. This means that you purchase a stock when its price in not only below or equal to your calculated fair price, but that it is considerably lower. This gives you a cushion where the assumptions regarding the company might be incorrect and the investment will be okay in the long-run (Battisti et al., 2019). The margin of safety means that your assumptions would have to be considerably wrong for the investment to fail. However, by diversifying your portfolio, the situation becomes statistical. For instance, if you invest in 15 firms, and only invest when a stock is lower than 15% of

your calculated intrinsic value, then two or three can go bad while the

entire portfolio will still perform splendidly.

Figure 9: *Description of Fair Value Vs. Stock Price.*

Fair Value Vs. Stock Price

Source: (Dividend Monk).

In the chart above, the best time to purchase would be when the stock price falls below the fair value. However, it is a difficult move since you cannot see the rest of the chart and the fair value is the calculated estimate of what the stock is worth rather than an absolute truth. By adhering to credible value investing principles, you can perform well since the chart shows that the fair value of a healthy business will be far less volatile than the stock price.

For you to purchase at an undervalued price, it is essential to know the fair price first. This requires a mixture of science and art. Science is used to determine company estimates and your expected rate of return, which are vital in calculating the objective fair value of the business. Art is used to handle the imperfect estimates which are based on historical growth rates and future trends. Here, the Discounted Cash Flow Analysis can be utilized since it a fundamental stock evaluation method for any asset or company that produces cash flows.

Value investing is often seen as a conservative investing technique. However, the primary aim of a margin of safety is to protect your return and to empower it. When you purchase a stock lower than the estimated fair value, the expectation is that the stock price will revert back to fair value in a rational market. When the growth expectations turn out to be correct and you purchased at an undervalued price, you will end up with a higher rate of return. On the other hand, the longer the stock remains undervalued, the more benefits shareholders get since their reinvested dividend continue to accumulate undervalued shares. An excellent example an individual who uses the margin of safety method is Warren Buffet. In his early days, Buffet did not invest in businesses expanding at an annual rate of 30-50%. Instead, he invested in companies that were profoundly undervalued. Rather of selecting large cap such as IBM, Buffet was a value investor who sought large mismatches between price and value. As his capital base expanded, it was not possible for Buffet to continue investing in small firms and he was forced to either purchase entire companies or invest primarily in huge caps.

There are two primary reasons for purchasing with a margin of safety. First, it makes the portfolio more conservative since your growth estimates might be a little bit off and the investment will be successful

(Battisti et al., 2019). Second, if the estimates are accurate, the rate of return will be higher since over time since the growth rate of investment is augmented by the extra fact that they were purchased at an undervalued price.

iii.   Avoid Dividend Traps

When searching for dividend stocks, it's tempting to incline towards securities with the utmost yields. This is not always the best approach; there's a lot more to a good dividend stock than a high yield. Dividends are frequently given by established firms, but dividends can also be utilized by troubled companies attempting to attract investors. A dividend trap, also known as a value trap, occurs when investor are lured by a high dividend return, only to discover that the investment was not great in the end.

Dividends are the income component of shareholder returns. Dividend yield is one of the oldest valuation methods. As such, dividend-paying stocks are frequently regarded as higher quality and more stable than non-dividend stocks. However, there is a point at which these stocks become riskier than the normal stock. Some deals are too good to be true. Consider a second-hand car dealer offering a huge discount on a vehicle you are interested in (Price, 2012). If the discount is too large, you begin to question the motives of the dealer. Although there are many stocks poised to offer a great return to investors, a large dividend yield mandates further investigation.

The first sign of a dividend trap is when a company is paying a much higher dividend return than its peers. When you come across such a scenario, do not just accept the face value. Instead, asses the company's capacity to meet its obligations and its management. If the stock continually drops or the firm is unable to pay the dividend as pledged, it is a value trap (Price, 2012). Here, you should asses the company's payout ratio, which is the amount of income going to dividend payments. A business that is paying out most of what it makes will be unable to sustain the dividend for long, and may be heading toward financial problems. Therefore, you should establish a baseline to determine if a stock has a high, low, or average dividend yield before investing.

The Importance of Precious Metals

Throughout history, precious metals have played an essential role in the global economy. Although the universal landscape has considerably changed since the commencement of the Gold Standard, precious metals still play a vital role in our financial future. Investors seeking a reliable investment can consider the precious metal investment. Unlike any other elements on earth, their distinct combination of brilliance, scarcity, durability, and utility infuse them with many economic purposes. Similarly, precious metals, such as gold, silver, platinum, and palladium, act as money, industrial products, and investment instruments throughout the global market (Shahid et.al, 2019). Consequently, this makes them a unique and practical investment option. Throughout the centuries, precious metals have been valued for their permanent value and a worldwide medium of exchange. At the same time, they have played a fundamental part in art and industry.

Precious metals are rare metals that have a high economic value because of multiple factors; scarcity, industrial uses, and as a store of value. The most popular precious metals for investors include gold, silver, and platinum. In the past, precious metals played a primary part in the global economy since numerous currencies were either minted utilizing these metals or back by them. Nonetheless, the situation has changed in the contemporary world and individuals can buy precious metals as financial assets. As an investment, precious metals are primarily used to diversify portfolios and as a store of value, specifically to hedge against volatility. For commercial purchases, precious metals are a vital component for commodities like electronics or jewelry.

Gold and silver are the most popular precious metals for investment aims. Those utilized in industrial activities include iridium, which is used in forte alloys, and palladium, which is utilized in chemical processes and electronics. Which precious metal is best for investment?

Gold is distinct because of its durability, malleability, and capacity to conduct both heat and electricity. Although it is primarily known as a store of value and for making jewelry, it has several industrial applications in electronics and dentistry. It is one of the most secure stores of value in any asset that one can invest in. Furthermore, the gold market is not affected by the supply and demand of other assets, which makes the metal a good investment during economic downturns. Gold prices have remained relatively stable despite the numerous crises that other markets across the world have had to endure (Shahid et.al, 2019). This is one of the primary reasons why individuals invest in gold and other metals. A gold investment allows the investor to have considerable control over their asset, especially in wherein the presence of market volatility.

Figure 10: *Historical prices of gold*

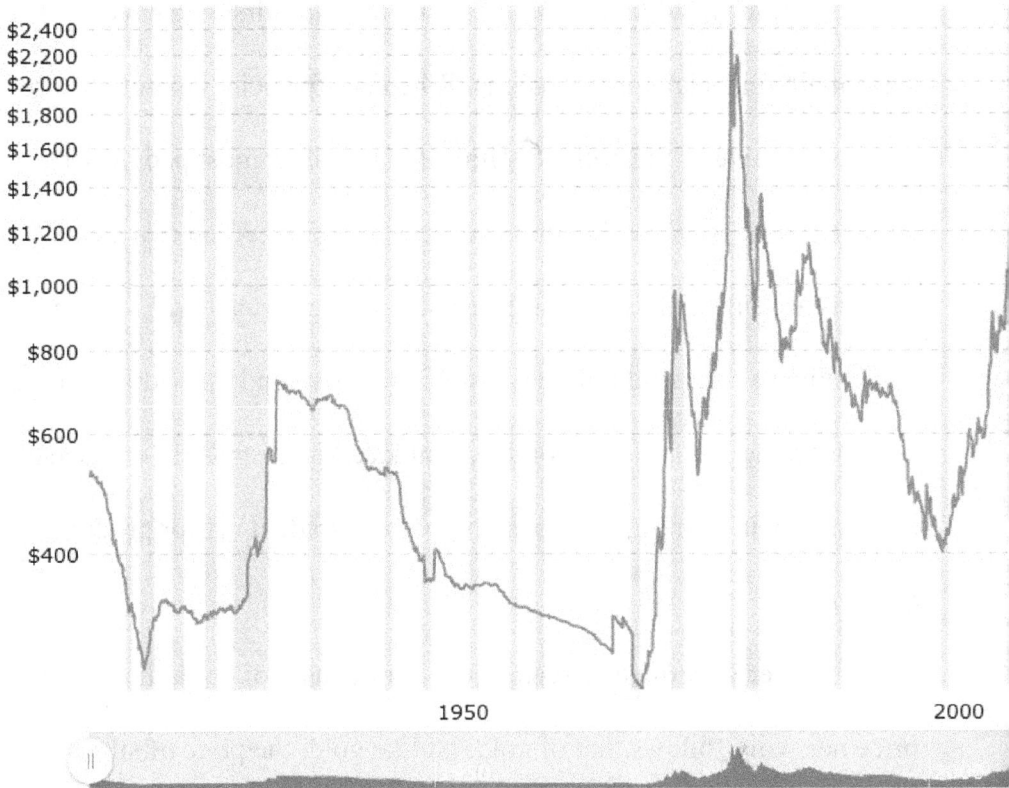

Source (Precious Metals Charts and Data | MacroTrends, n.d.)

The value of gold is determined by the market throughout the week. The prices of gold are less impacted by the forces of supply and demand because the new mine supply is massively overshadowed by the amount of hoarded gold. This means that when hoarders want to sell, the price drops, and when they want to purchase, a new supply is absorbed and gold prices increase (Hammoudeh, Malik & McAleer,

2011). Various factors increase the value of gold. First, we have systematic financial apprehensions. When the financial institutions are seen as unstable or the political climate is unstable, most people seek gold as a store of value. Second, we have inflation. When real estate markets are suffering, investors normally seek gold as it will retain its value. Finally, war and political instability often send individuals into a gold-hoarding mode (Hammoudeh, Malik & McAleer, 2011). A person can store their entire life savings on gold and trade it off for products and services.

Silver is frequently seen as the poor cousin of gold, though its price normally follows that of gold. Unlike gold, the price of silver fluctuates between its apparent role as a store of value and as an industrial component. As a result, the price fluctuations of silver are volatile than gold. In the last year, most financial experts stipulate that silver has outperformed gold (Hammoudeh, Malik & McAleer, 2011). In addition, silver is one of the most popular options when investing in precious metals. Apart from having multiple uses in many industries, silver is more volatile because of its demand. Although most people see silver as less desirable than gold, it can be more reliant in a prosperous economy, where the demand for metal is high. Irrespective of silver`s

higher volatility, it is viewed as a hedge against inflation.

Figure 11: *Historical prices for silver*

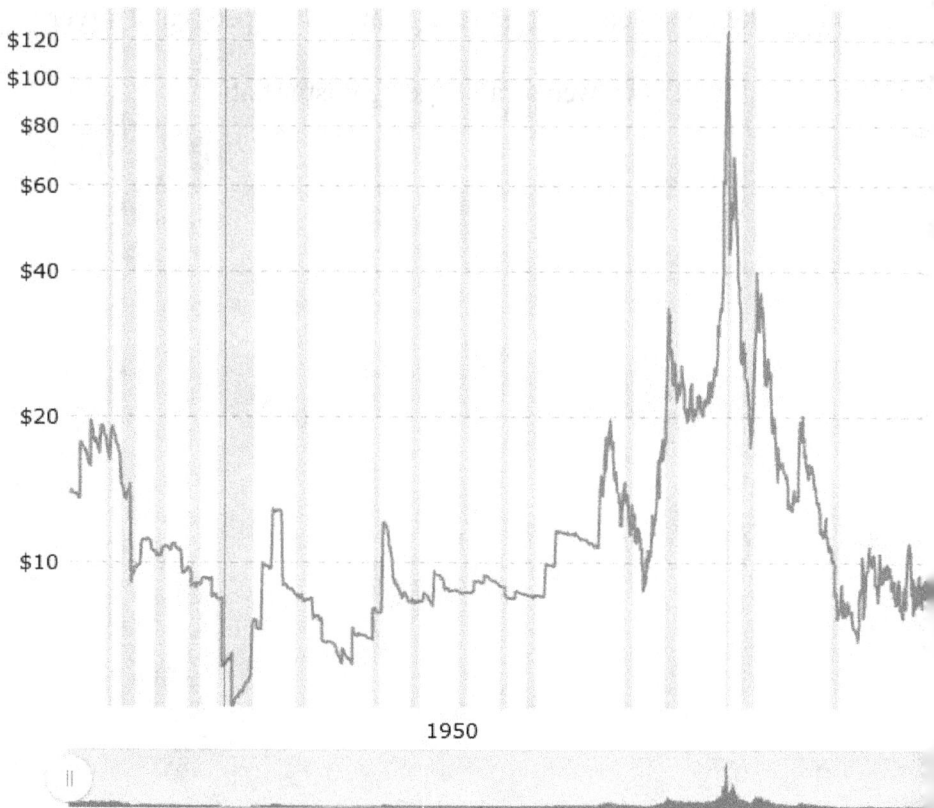

Source (Precious Metals Charts and Data | MacroTrends, n.d.)

Although silver trades inline gold as a precious commodity, its industrial use exerts an equally strong effect on its price. Silver is used in various industries including the photography sector to make silver-based photographic film. Furthermore, the rise of a huge middle class in developing countries in the East and Africa has created an escalated demand for electrical gadgets, medical equipment, and other products that require silver as a raw material (Hammoudeh, Malik & McAleer, 2011). Similarly, silver is used in superconductor applications and microcircuit markers. Currently, it is not clear if, or the degree to which these innovations will impact the overall non-investment demand for silver.

Apart from gold and silver, another precious metal that is ideal to invest in is platinum. It is traded in the global commodities market. It tends to have a greater price than gold during normal times and political stability since it is rarer. Only a small amount of platinum is mined annually. Despite having higher prices than gold, platinum is not prevalent among investors due to its rarity and scarcity.

Figure 12: *Historical Prices of Platinum*

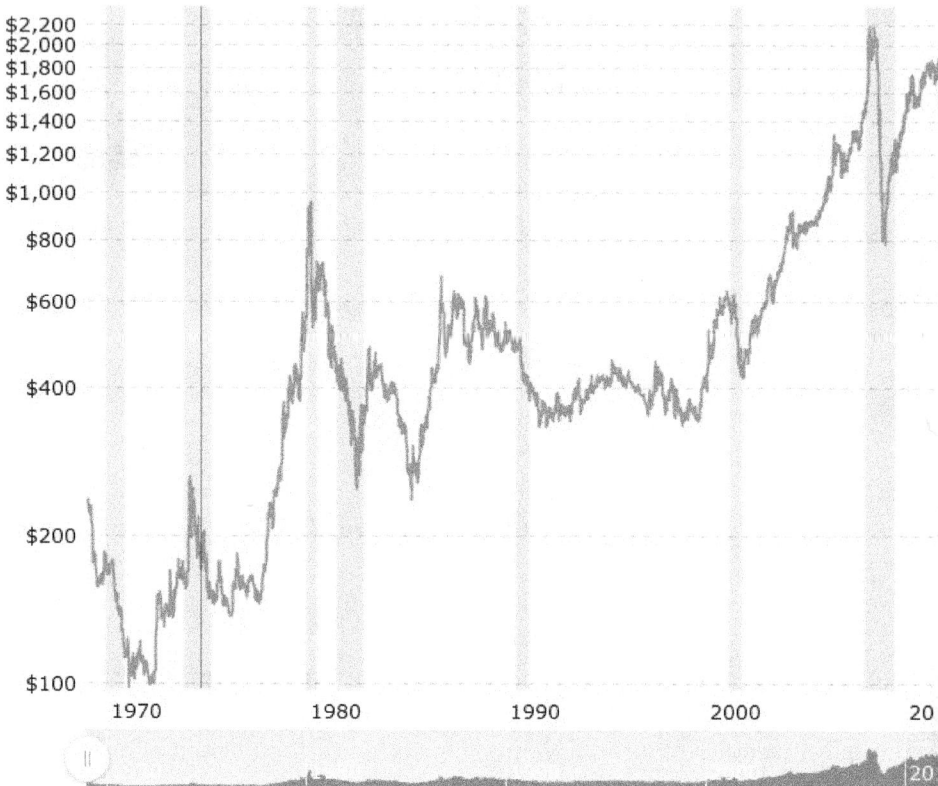

Source (Precious Metals Charts and Data | MacroTrends, n.d.)

Various factors affect platinum`s price. Platinum is an industrial component and its greatest demand comes from the automotive sector. The metal is a fundamental constitute in catalytic converters, which are used to minimize destructive emissions. Jewellery follows, and then the petroleum and computer industries follow. Due to the automobile's heavy dependence on platinum, its prices are influenced primarily by vehicle sales and production. Today, increasing legislation is mandating car manufacturers to implement more catalytic converters, raising demand. Another factor that affects platinum`s demand is the fact that platinum mines are concentrated in only two nations; South Africa and Russia (Hammoudeh, Malik & McAleer, 2011). As a result, this creates a more likelihood for cartel-like behavior that would back or artificially increase platinum prices. Therefore, platinum`s rarity combine with its vast industrial use, makes it an appealing investment alternative to competing assets such as stocks, bonds, and currencies.

One of the lesser-known and underrated precious metals is palladium, which has more industrial uses. Palladium is a shiny, silvery metal utilized in numerous manufacturing processes, especially in electronic and industrial commodities. The metal can also be utilized in medicine, chemical processes, jewellery, and groundwater treatment. The supply of platinum is rare and it is mined in the United States, Canada, Russia, and South Africa. Close to 50% of the planet`s supply of palladium comes from Russia (Hammoudeh, Malik & McAleer, 2011). Palladium was first incorporated into jewelry in 1939. Here, palladium was mixed with yellow gold to form an alloy stronger than white gold. The metal can create thin sheets up to one-two hundredth fifty-thousandths of an inch. It is malleable but becomes stronger and harder when worked at room temperature. These sheets are utilized to make fuel cells and solar energy. The primary usage of palladium is in catalytic converters. Palladium is much harder than platinum, making the element more durable than platinum.

How do you invest in precious metals? Investors looking to add precious metals to their portfolios have various ways of realizing that. Those who prefer to hold these metals directly can buy physical bullion, like bars or minted coins, and store them in safety deposit boxes. For individuals anticipating the worst, bullion is the only choice, but for those with a time horizon, bullion is illiquid and hard to maintain (Shahid et.al, 2019). This is a direct approach of ownership that minimizes counterparty risk but incurs more costs because of insurance and storage. Another approach is to purchase future contracts for the specific metal or to purchase shares in publicly traded firms involved in the exploration or production of these metals. In addition, mutual funds and exchange-traded funds provide many approaches, such as money backed by bullion and leveraged exposure. However, exchange-traded funds do not provide you access to the physical product, which means that you do not have a claim on the metal in the fund. Another method is through future and option markets which offer liquidity and leverage to investors who wish to place huge bets on precious metals (Shahid et.al, 2019). Finally, certificates give investors all the advantages of physical ownership of the metal without the trouble of mobility and storage. For those looking for insurance during a crisis, certificates are the ideal approach.

Every investment has its unique risks. Despite leveraging some level of security, investing in precious metals is a risk. Prices can plummet during recessions, forcing investors to liquidate their assets to cover their expenses. At the same time, physical assets can be hard to dispose of at reasonable prices, especially during periods of increased volatility. Finally, precious metals have an extra risk of being stolen when stored in the house. However, during economic uncertainty, the prices of precious metals escalate, benefitting sellers.

The primary reason to invest in precious metals is because of demand and scarcity. Like other natural resources, the mining of these metals will decline until they are depleted. They are not infinite. At the same time, the demand for precious metals continues to increase as consumer applications increase. Hence, acquiring gold and silver bullion today will augment your probability of having extremely valuable resources in the future. Another reason for investing in precious metals is liquidity. The problem with having a house is that you cannot dispose of it when in need of quick cash. Although most assets have value, the complete process of disposing of them is cumbersome, making it difficult for people to sell them. However, precious metals are easy to sell.

Moreover, investing in precious metals diversified a portfolio and helps keep a healthy balance between physical and stock assets. In 2008, many people in the United States lost their investments and assets because of the financial recession. In such times, precious metal investment is vital to holding a stable financial portfolio. If individuals had invested in these metals, they could have mitigated some of their losses during the financial crisis. Therefore, it is better to be prepared for an economic crisis by investing in precious metals. Furthermore, precious metals are a haven against the dollar. The US dollar is continually doing up because of inflation, while precious metals increase in value. As of 2019, the US owes China more than $22 trillion (Shahid et.al, 2019). Since the value of the dollar is based on the fact that the US has pledged to pay back its debts. This means that in case of another crisis, the value of the dollar could be obliterated and people would require a backup to maintain financial protection. The haven is precious metals since they also safeguard against inflation.

Additionally, precious metals are easily purchased from bullion traders, market dealers, and banks. Apart from the easy access, these metals are abundant in the markets, which mean one can acquire one with the correct resource and adequate knowledge about them. The primary advantage of investing in precious metals is their economic price. Investors can possess these metals and they have a wide range of options to select from when investing. For example, investors with a difficult time investing in a full ounce of metal like gold can still opt for other more affordable precious metals such as silver. Furthermore, the demand for precious metals, like gold and silver has surged in the previous year. Regardless of the numerous economic uncertainties and market volatilities, the demand for silver and gold has continued to increase compared to other precious metals.

Precious metals provide distinct inflationary safety because they have inherent value, have no credit risk, and cannot be inflated. In addition, they provide genuine insurance against financial or political turmoil. From an investment perspective, precious metals offer low or negative correlation to other asset categories such as bonds and stocks. As such, even a tiny portion of these metals in your portfolio will minimize volatility and risk. This shows that precious metals offer a practical way of diversifying a portfolio. The primary aspect is to understand your financial goals and risk profile before investing.

References

A Guide to High-risk Investments. (n.d.). SyndicateRoom.

https://www.syndicateroom.com/alternative-investments/high-

risk-investments

Apergis, N., Hayat, T., & Saeed, T. (2021). US partisan conflict

uncertainty and oil prices. *Energy Policy, 150,* 112118.

Armantier, O., Koşar, G., Pomerantz, R., Skandalis, D., Smith, K.,

Topa, G., & Van der Klaauw, W. (2021). How economic crises

affect inflation beliefs: Evidence from the Covid-19 pandemic.

Journal of Economic Behavior & Organization, 189, 443-469.

Battisti, E., Miglietta, N., Salvi, A., & Creta, F. (2019). Strategic

approaches to value investing: a systematic literature review of

international studies. Review of International Business and

Strategy.

Brittney. (2021). Dave Ramsey Budget Percentages. Retrieved from

https://makesavespendgive.com/dave-ramsey-budget-

percentages/

How to use a Margin of Safety when Investing. (n.d). Dividend Monk.
Retrieved from https://www.dividendmonk.com/margin-of-safety/

Fabozzi, F. J., & Markowitz, H. M. (Eds.). (2011). The theory and
practice of investment management: Asset allocation, valuation,
portfolio construction, and strategies (Vol. 198). John Wiley &
Sons.

Guerard Jr, J. B. (Ed.). (2009). Handbook of portfolio construction:
contemporary applications of Markowitz techniques. Springer
Science & Business Media.

Gutkevych, S., & Vikhliaiev, M. (2021). Risks In Investing. Baltic
Journal of Economic Studies, 7(3), 82-87.

Hammoudeh, S., Malik, F., & McAleer, M. (2011). Risk management
of precious metals. The Quarterly Review of Economics and
Finance, 51(4), 435-441.

Hardyman, R. (2017). Understanding Stocks and Investing. The Rosen
Publishing Group, Inc.

Hillier, D., Draper, P., & Faff, R. (2006). Do precious metals shine? An investment perspective. Financial Analysts Journal, 62(2), 98-106.

Hunjra, A. I., Alawi, S. M., Colombage, S., Sahito, U., & Hanif, M. (2020). Portfolio Construction by Using Different Risk Models: A Comparison among Diverse Economic Scenarios. Risks, 8(4), 126.

Lee, S. C., & Eid, W. (2018). Portfolio construction and risk management: theory versus practice. RAUSP Management Journal, 53, 345-365.

Long, T. (2016). Serving up a budgeting pie will help youth stay financially healthy. Retrieved from https://www.canr.msu.edu/news/serving_up_a_budgeting_pie_will_help_youth_stay_financially_healthy

Nguyen, L., Gallery, G., & Newton, C. (2019). The joint influence of financial risk perception and risk tolerance on individual investment decision-making. Accounting & Finance, 59, 747-771.

Nofsinger, J. R. (2017). The psychology of investing. Routledge.

Philavong, M., & Phomvongsa, S. (2021). Cryptocurrency Business
Covers the Psychological Impact of the Business Market on the
Youth Segment. *Journal of Asian Multicultural Research for
Economy and Management Study, 2*(2), 35-39.

Portfolio Construction. (n.d). Invest Blue. Retrieved from
https://www.investblue.com.au/belief-5-portfolio-construction

Price, J. (2012). Return on equity traps and how to avoid them. Equity,
26(3), 4-6.

Royal, J. (2021, August 1). 8 Best Low-Risk Investments in March
2020. Bankrate. https://www.bankrate.com/investing/low-risk-
investments/

Russo, A. (2013). Low risk equity Investments: Empirical evidence,
theories, and the Amundi experience." (pp. 1-32). Amundi
Working Paper WP-033-2013.

Shahid, M. N., Jehanzeb, M., Abbas, A., Zubair, A., & Akbar, M. A. H. (2019). Predictability of precious metals and adaptive market hypothesis. International Journal of Emerging Markets.

Vayas-Ortega, G., Soguero-Ruiz, C., Rojo-Álvarez, J. L., & Gimeno-Blanes, F. J. (2020). On the differential analysis of enterprise valuation methods as a guideline for unlisted companies assessment (I): Empowering discounted cash flow valuation. Applied Sciences, 10(17), 5875.

www.ingramcontent.com/pod-product-compliance
Lightning Source LLC
Chambersburg PA
CBHW050212270326
41914CB00003BA/377